CROSSROADS VII

POETRY AND PROSE BY
CENTRAL VIRGINIA TEENS

SPRING 2019

TUPELO PRESS
TEEN WRITING CENTER

The views and opinions expressed in this anthology are solely those of the original authors, and do not reflect policy or position of any associated schools or organizations.

Student Editors:

Editor-in-Chief: Baylina Pu
Senior Editors: Rachel Beling, Mary Dwyer, Chloe Whaley
Editors: Abigail Connelly, Stella Rowe
Junior Editor: Natasha Levine
Managing Editor: Rachel Beling

Participating Schools:

Monticello High School
Charlottesville High School
Albemarle High School
Western Albemarle High School
Covenant School
St. Anne's Belfield
Tandem Friends
Louisa High School
The Miller School

Book Design by Max March

© 2019 Tupelo Press Teen Writing Center
All rights reserved.

Published by the Tupelo Press Teen Writing Center.

Dedication

to Writerhouse for six years of faithful support

"The ornament of a house is the friends who frequent it."
—Ralph Waldo Emerson

Foreword

Within these covers, live a delightful representation of local teen poems and prose, lovingly curated by eight student editors. This year saw our highest submissions ever, our editors chose the contents before you from one hundred and sixty submissions, a welcome sign that creative writing is thriving among our area high school teens. Each year our editors are confronted by the call of unique tones and styles of submissions, asked to weave together incredibly disparate writing. It brings me great joy to watch our student editors sift through the work, listening to the voices rising from the page, combining prose and poetry into the anthology you hold.

This year saw more experimental and hybrid work than ever. It's an incredible challenge and feat to put together an anthology of this size and scope in a mere month and a half between our end of submissions and our deadline to go to print, and to do so with minimal changes to each author's vision. Our editors put in long hours, much thought and care, and our book designer, Max March, has applied his magic (and a great deal of patience, without which this book couldn't exist). We are grateful to Proal Heartwell for his passion for student writing in our community, for founding the Prose and Poetry Contest over two decades ago, and for selecting our readers. We thank Camille Dungy for selecting our winning writer, and for Writerhouse for giving our program and our young writers a home for the past seven years. We thank St. Anne's Belfield for hosting our ceremony and for their good care.

One perk of an editorial team is to have a little license and fun with the theme and design. We like a little mystery! Each year the flow of the anthology lends to some natural divisions, and our editors share those this year with printers ornaments at the top of each page that change with the themes in the writing. We'll announce the meaning behind those ornaments on our website on Saturday, March 23rd, the day after our Mirabella reading and award ceremony.

In this, our seventh year of publication and readings, the most important part of our program is our students, and in their writing lies the hope for our future. Enjoy, and our great thanks for reading along.

Mirabella
Prose & Poetry Contest

Sponsored by St. Anne's Belfield,
Albemarle High School Creative Writing Pathways,
and the Tupelo Press Teen Writing Center

High School Prose and Poetry Contest Winners

see, i told you i loved you
Maya Goldstein

Clean Cut
Ava Martin

Al Hudaydah
Kiran Klubock-Shukla

The Secret of Mankind
Elizabeth Davis

The Radioactive Ghost of Kilkenny
James O'Brien

A First Goodbye
Cassie Hersman

Nuclear
Mary Dwyer

Rusting
Brehanu Bugg

cyborg symphony
Stella Rowe

Days in the Circus
Aoife Arras

Quiet Kitchen
Damien Heller-Chen

Rattlesnake Reveries
Abigail Connelly

Growing Up
Maddie Kwasnick

Ecstatic Fragmentation
Bryn Malone

Lullaby
Tina Feng

Aphrodite in Birth & Death
Astrid Weisend

the garden
Chloe Whaley

disharmonious
Eliza Sanusi

This is Hell
Cesca Grazioli

Santa, God, and a Ten-Year-Old
Hannah Fowler

Crossroads VII Writing Contest:
Sponsored by The Tupelo Press Teen Writing Center

Judged by Camille Dungy, Professor at Colorado State University, recipient of an American Book Award, two Northern California Book Awards, two NAACP Image Award nominations, and two Hurston/Wright Legacy Award nominations.

Winner:
Cicadas
Baylina Pu

Runner-up:
snow night on the dead end
Meridith Carter Frazee

Finalists:

Remember Us This Way
Emily Garcia

concertos
Aimee Straka

snow night on the dead end
Meridith Carter Frazee

Cicadas
Baylina Pu

Cyclicality
Charlotte Walters

Pale-lunged
Rachel Beling

Walking the Neighborhood
Iris Papin

Melting Sabbath
Hewson Duffy

sometimes I forget I knew you
Johanna Hall

anxiety and religion in eleven parts
McKenzie Hall

Table of Contents

Quiet Kitchen *Damien Heller-Chen* 13
The Parkway *Prentice McNeely* 14
Remember Us This Way *Emily Garcia* 16
Reverie *Rachel Schweitzer* 17
Head Wounds and Heartthrobs *Henry Kipps* 18
cyborg symphony *Stella Rowe* 22
Life Between Two Worlds *Virginia Smith* 23
Santa, God, and a Ten-Year-Old *Hannah Fowler* 24
Sweet Sensations *Nyah Catherine-Lim* 26
snow night on the dead end *Meridith Carter Frazee* 28
disharmonious *Eliza Sanusi* 30
Clean Cut *Ava Martin* 32
Lullaby *Tina Feng* 34
Virginia I'll Miss You *Dawson Dickerson* 35
Nuclear *Mary Dwyer* 36
Hidden Gravel Roads *Madilyn Glaser* 37
To My Yellow Mimi *Ela Singleton* 39
Big Goofy Smile *Son Kim* 40
Tobias *Tylar Schmitt* 42
Grown Up *Maddie Kwasnick* 46
Ode to the Internet *Hewson Duffy* 48
Cyclicality *Charlotte Walters* 50
see, i told you i loved you. *Maya Goldstein* 52
The Beauty in Everything *Lindsay King* 53
The Room *Youjia Yang* 55
Father *Nola Ralls* 57
Warmth *Robin Guziejka* 58
A father *Ari Pyle* 60

Amaya Rose *LaShalle Schornberg* 61
But You Didn't *Nora Li* 62
The Fire *Aaron Osborne* 65
Sanguine *Miriam Topchyan* 68
A Letter From Hope *Sarah Swagerl*. 70
Last Conversation with Grandfather *Trent Moran* 73
Crash *Jenna DiGirolamo*. 74
Voices of the Dark *Stevie Tyree* 76
The Three Strangers *Maddie Kwasnick* 78
Walking the Neighborhood *Iris Papin* 80
A Wednesday Night *Danie Leyshon* 81
sometimes I forget I knew you *Johanna Hall* 82
The War We Wage *Bailey Logan*. 84
Our Soldiers *Corin Saint Ours*. 86
Hope *Matthew Farina*. 88
Al Hudaydah *Kiran Klubock-Shukla* 90
South Sudan *Isaac Francis* 91
The Word *Andy Packwood* 93
Radioactive Ghost of Kilkenny *James O'Brien*. 96
Not More, But Why *Yndeiah Kilby* 98
My God, My God, I Forsake You *Jennifer Bui* 100
Unknown *Lily Van Liew*. 102
anxiety and religion in eleven parts *McKenzie Hall* 104
This is Hell *Cesca Grazioli* 107
The Evil Lake *Lily Deleo*. 110
Stars and Streetlights / Man on the Moon *Rafe Forward*. 113
The Moon's Beckoning *David Colavincenzo* 114
Aphrodite in Birth & Death *Astrid Weisend*. 117
ecstatic fragmentation *Bryn Malone*. 120
Willow's Deal *Henry Kipps* 121
Rattlesnake Reveries *Abigail Connelly*. 125
concertos *Aimee Straka* 126

Days in the Circus *Aoife Arras* 128
Living in a Broken World *Ashley Taylor* 131
Rusting *Brehanu Bugg* 133
Sea-Song *Kathryn Stenburgh* 134
I'm a Grenade *Bailey Logan* 137
Cicadas *Baylina Pu* 139
A First Goodbye *Cassie Hersman* 141
The Nailbiter *Anna Dove* 144
symphonies *Aimee Straka* 146
Curvature: A Triptych for the Spine *Johanna Hall* 148
Ode to Sentences *Meridith Frazee*. 151
Caged *Alena Masloff*. 153
pale-lunged *Rachel Beling* 154
The Garden *Chloe Whaley* 156
Self-Worth *Sabrina Whearty*. 158
A Letter to My Parents as I'm Turning 19 *Long Hoang* 159
I Hope *Catherine Paphites* 162
Melting Sabbath *Hewson Duffy* 163
Clarisse *Niav Condren*. 165
growing pains *Maryam Alwan* 167
a list *McKenzie Hall* 169

Quiet Kitchen
Damien Heller-Chen

A silent night atop a table high,
A small mouse settles down and gazes up,
The mouse stares out the window at the sky,
As water drops drip from faucet to cup.
A quiet night the kitchen lies serene,
A cat dozes off, her job clear as day,
This simple task ignored to lick and preen,
As the old hinges creak in the doorway.
With the street still busy, even past dark,
People carry on smoking, or walking,
Streets and buildings shrink til they're a mere mark,
Hearing the faint sounds of small men talking.
As an ink drop falls from an artist's pen,
Only the artist decides where and when.

The Parkway
Prentice McNeely

Rolling down the road
Windows down
Sweltering hot air battering my face
Memory lane peering in the rearview

Nostrils filled with fresh air
Mother's perfume
Father's old hat
And exhaust fumes

"Sweet Home" billowing from the stereo
"Summer Breeze" on repeat
Steady drone of the exhaust filling empty space
Conversation slight but nothing needs saying

Mountains below
Sky and heaven above
Clouds and sun shadow overhead
Road slicing through mountainous forest

Spearmint overwhelming taste buds
In attempts to eclipse the coffee
Masking the once distinct smelling egg
And hiding remnants of toast

No one for miles
People scarce and distant
The Mustang returning to nature
The place it had been before

Palm resting on the gear shift at five
Speed sitting easy at 52 as the trees pass by
Temperature at 72
Humidity high
Fuel at 3 quarters

Engulfed in leather
Protected by steel
And the cross hanging from the rear view
The rubber between passengers and asphalt

Sun beginning to set
Dawn approaching dusk
Journey nearing end
Destination closing in

Stomachs empty
Appetites high
The need for nature and nurture compete
Outcome of battle imminent

Unwinding the mountain
Falling victim to nurture and night
Fuel of car and body diminished

Remember Us This Way

Emily Garcia

& In the silence of a gray room
The colors speak to me, the way a mother reads to her child
Making me come to my senses after years of blindness
If I ever leave, I'll miss you Virginia

Rolling hills of emerald green, orange & yellow
Watercolor sunsets handpainted in the sky
Scenery I wish to hold in the palm of my hand
& have people I've never met dancing on my fingertips

If I ever leave, I'll miss you Virginia
For crossing my path with beautiful souls
Because of all the places in this world, in this unfathomably large universe
You let them remain here. With you.

If I ever leave, I'll miss you Virginia
For holding my hand when I stumbled to the ground
& housing my broken heart between mountaintops
You pulled me into your lap & told me that the good and the bad
    are temporary

If I ever leave, I'll miss you Virginia
For housing last moments
Like the tired sloppy love confessions we let slip from our lips at 5am
The time we sat on old sofas and talked endlessly about what could be

I will forever hold these thoughts in the frame of my mind
In the silence of my own gray room.

Reverie

Rachel Schweitzer

From black and white burst a world of color. She let her eyes flutter to a close. Her mind, her heart opened with a crack, and life poured into the sky. It danced from her fingertips, spilled from her gaping mouth.

Faint notes played, resting on her skin, sleeping in her bones. Vibrancy in the air, swift lines and milky hues, painting creation.

    A soft melody, drifting along pastel spirits.

    An exhale and a storm erupting of pigment, streaming from unconscious, liquid wishes.

Ecstatic ribbons surge in all directions from her sinking being.

A crescendo of song, roaring octaves and thundering disorder. Electric perception, tumultuous.

Silence, underlying and stark grey lines of structure. Eyes, mind awake.

Head Wounds and Heartthrobs

Henry Kipps

Mary was confused. She was standing in the bedroom of Samantha Kiri, who was lying heavily on her bed, the sheets splattered with blood. Mary's arm was outstretched, her revolver smoking in her hands. The room reeked of gore and gunpowder.

"Ugh, that was a trip," Samantha groaned, pressing her palm against her bloody forehead. "What the hell was that for?"

"What's going on here?" Mary asked. "Why aren't you dead?"

Samantha got up to her feet, pointing an accusing finger at Mary. "Oh, no, you're not the one who gets to ask the questions here. You ruined my bed!"

"I *shot* you in the *head!*" Mary hissed.

"Yes, you did," Samantha said, arms crossed. "And it hurt. A *lot.*"

"Why aren't you dead?" Mary repeated. "Answer me!"

"Why should I? I'm not the one who broke into my house and put a bullet through my skull. Do you know what that does to a person?"

"Yes!" Mary exclaimed. "It kills them! Or at least it's *supposed to!*"

Samantha rolled her eyes. "Well, as far as I care, you weren't *supposed* to shoot me. What's your deal? I never did anything to you."

Mary grit her teeth, keeping her gun at the ready. "I'm an assassin. Freelance."

Samantha's eyes widened. "Oh. Ooooooh. I'm sorry."

Mary's vice grip on her revolver loosened, causing the barrel to dip towards the ground. Her brow furrowed. "Excuse me?"

"Well, it's just, you were hired for an impossible job. That can't be fun."

"I'm not sure I follow."

"I don't die," she said, like it was the most normal thing in the world.

Mary narrowed her eyes. "Come again?"

"I don't die. Simple as that."

"What? No. People don't just not die."

Samantha rolled her eyes. "You shot me twice in the head, and here we are. What more proof do you need?"

"Okay, fine, you don't die. Why?"

Samantha shrugged. "I've always been like this."

Mary clutched at her head. This was infuriating. What was she supposed to do if the target was freaking *immortal?* Had her client known?

She took a deep breath and turned back to Samantha. "Alright, question. How many people are in on this?"

"I don't know, a few?" She scratched her head. "Not many. It… doesn't come up that often."

"Christopher Phillips?"

Samantha started. "How do you—oh, don't tell me that he—"

Mary's hand clenched, the hard metal of the gun digging into her skin. "Hired me," she finished.

Samantha leaned backwards, breathing in through clenched teeth, and collapsed onto the sticky, reddened comforter behind her. Mary sat down on the writing desk pushed against the wall and dropped the revolver onto a stack of papers next to her.

This was a mess.

Christopher Phillips was an old friend of hers. He worked for one of the… lesser known branches of government, and was a frequent client. Samantha Kiri had been an odd target, certainly, but she hadn't questioned it—she didn't pry into Chris's business, and he didn't pry into hers. Respecting each other's secrets was the only way they could function as friends, considering their professions. But why would he send her to kill someone he knew couldn't die? It didn't make sense!

Maybe Samantha had answers. "So how do you know Chris?"

Samantha took a few seconds to respond. "He was the guy who showed up at my door when the government found out about the whole 'can't die' thing. We got to know each other, he started dating my roommate Ellie, we all became friends… I don't know why he'd send someone to kill me, though. Unless…" Samantha turned narrowed eyes onto Mary. "Long brown hair, hazel eyes, kinda short… oh, for god's sake!"

"What are you talking about?"

"Chris and Ellie's one year relationship 'anniversary' was a few days ago, and the conversation somehow got around to my own romantic life, and—"

"Oh my god." Mary grimaced, her mind racing back to the previous day

"Hey, Chris. Is this a business call?"

"Yes, but before that, I've got a question for you. Sorry if this is a bit unexpected, but are you dating anyone?"

Mary froze for a second. "You're not asking me out, right? 'Cause you know I'm—"

"No!" he blurted. "No, sorry, no, not at all. Just wondering. So, are you?"

"No. I've kinda stopped looking."

"Oh?"

"Surprisingly enough, there aren't a lot of girls willing to date trained killers. It's like, if they could just get past that, maybe there'd be something, but, I mean, I understand. I'd be scared of me too, if I were, you know, normal."

"If only there was a girl who wasn't *scared of you, right?"*

Mary laughed. "If only. As I said, I've stopped looking."

He chuckled. "So, anyway. There's this Samantha Kiri…"

Back in the present, that very same Samantha was still talking. "—so I said, 'oh, she'd have brown hair, hazel eyes, she wouldn't be taller than me, and she'd be chill with immortality.' And it was a joke, I mean mostly, you know, but here we are anyway."

Mary slammed her head into the desk as hard as she could. "This. Is the stupidest. Blind date. Ever."

"I know, right?" Samantha said. "I swear, the next time I see him…"

Mary sighed. "I'm really sorry. I can't imagine this is how you wanted to spend your evening." She glanced towards Samantha. "But, I mean, since we're here and all."

She nodded, blushing. "Right. I mean…"

"Yeah. So. Um." Mary coughed. "Wanna, maybe, get lunch some time?"

"Uh, sounds great. How about Friday? You already know where I live and stuff, so…"

"Cool. Um." Mary holstered her revolver and got to her feet. "I'll get Chris to reimburse you for the bedsheets."

"Thanks," she laughed. "Friday, then?"

Mary smiled. "Yep. And this time, maybe I'll do a better job blowing you away."

cyborg symphony
Stella Rowe

today someone told me:
  "if you're lonely, it's only because you just sit and watch the sky through your window,
    barely passing time. you'd find there's a world waiting for you to escape your sullen mind –
    maybe if you would find the acute strength to lace up your shoes, watch for mud, and go outside."
   and so i embarked on a scavenger hunt. but at the end of this search i found only myself (you see,
   i was *actually* seeking something else).
   myself has these leaping eyes warping wide
   with thoughts barely visualized.
   they leave her when they've echoed enough, to become steam.
   she closes the tight doors of reality behind her & just misses a dream.
   then, the dizzy pasts go from vapor to stratus clouds, so she says "hello up there!" before they
   come cascading down on this small outstretched body preparing to drown.

a reflection gleams in the pool at my feet:
a face of frigid droplets frees a voice so sweet until
its rhythm waves me into a familiar dance,
on a narrow-set street overflowing in a trance and looming tall.
letting distant recollections sway,
sinking deep into the walls.

Life Between Two Worlds
Virginia Smith

Pictures float throughout the room
Cradling emotions, both longing and sadness.
Posters plaster the walls, the floor
Revealing her life before
Before she struggled, now lost in a mix of cultures.
Portraits hang, revealing her family, her old life
But also her new life, trying to disguise what used to be.
But nothing erases her memories
A room divided by a curtain, two sides:
One side that is seen through a foreigner, a stranger's eye
Where nothing is familiar, relatable,
Cold objects, meaningless to anyone but her.
But another side, private and hidden, memories kept close to herself,
Afraid she will lose them to her new home.
Drawn back, the curtain of privacy reveals much more.
Reflections that crack through every spot on the floor and wall,
Begging to be noticed, begging to be recognized
Glimpses into her family life that bring back joy.
Her heritage shines through with a sense of deep pride
Immersing visitors in a culture far from their own.
The struggle of belonging is suddenly gone.
These memories overflow, reflecting her other life
The life that defines her, makes her who she is.
Pictures are worth a thousand words, but her memories are worth much more.

Santa, God, and a Ten-Year-Old
Hannah Fowler

"You *have* to tell me," I insisted, tears welling up in my eyes, "is Santa real?"

My mother put down her trowel. I had walked outside in flip-flops to confront her while she was gardening.

"Well," she sighed, knowing this was the end of an era, "I think you know the answer if you're asking me."

Darn. That put a damper on a Tuesday afternoon. I was so mad. Since a ten-year-old cannot do much to revolt against the enablers of this conspiracy, I settled for storming off to angrily watch cartoons.

First the Tooth Fairy, now *this*?! What else were they lying about? Soon, I found myself writing down all of my default beliefs: Santa, the Tooth Fairy, the Easter Bunny, God, and democracy. Going through the list, I crossed off everything involving holidays, but figured I could leave democracy for now. After all, I *was* only ten. For a moment, I paused, staring at "God," written in blue crayon. I had never questioned this before, and had never thought of what might happen if I stopped believing.

My family has never been particularly religious. We went to services on major holidays, but there was no pre-dinner prayer, Church camp, nor Sunday school (after taking more than my fair share of snacks, I couldn't show my gluttonous face around *there* anymore). Regardless of a clear absence of religious influence, I *did* believe in God. Once or twice, I even *prayed* to try and test the theory. The results were inconclusive, so I shrugged it off and continued on with my life. But *now*, I couldn't trust *anything* or *anyone*. If Santa was just an illusion to make children happy, what if God was the adult equivalent? Oh my gosh, was *everything* a lie?! Soon, I began berating my parents with questions about their personal religious beliefs. I was met with "I don't know," and "what do *you* think?"

Following two weeks of deliberation, I reached a conclusion. Confidently, I marched into my room, grabbed my list, and crossed off "God," this time using black sharpie. I felt liberated, like I could take on the world with a new, mature perspective. In parallel, I felt exponentially smaller. I had just rejected the idea of a "greater purpose."

Through my new atheist lense, I discovered that I did not trust many people. I was baffled. An existential crisis triggered by finding out the truth about Santa had made me abandon my belief in God. Great. *Santa* was the root of my trust issues. Seems reasonable for a ten-year-old. Oh well. At least I still had democracy. That is, until I asked my mother what "gerrymandering" meant…

Sweet Sensations

Nyah Catherine-Lim

At the dining room table
An aroma of sweet cranberry orange sauce and buttery mashed potatoes fills my nose
Leaving me with a sensation I get once a year
Plates and knives clatter as my sister and I set the table
Burgundy napkins with embroidered brown leaves are placed right on top of the plates
My grandpa is the one to sit down last
Once we all gather together
The passing of food begins
Every year my grandpa tells the same stories and my uncle and aunt ask me the same questions
How's school?
What sports are you playing for the winter?
The answers are still the same
One joke after another
I have enough cheesy topics for a lifetime
No topic of life imaginable is left undiscussed
Religion, sports, politics, and grizzly bears are just a few of the many random topics talked about
Mashed potatoes are almost gone
I always fill my stomach to the maximum on this holiday
But make sure to save some room for pie and ice cream
Sometimes pumpkin
Rarely blueberry
This year's was apple (my favorite)
It's out of the oven now
Hot but the smell is mouthwatering

People are full but don't want to miss an exceptional pastry sitting in front of them
It doesn't take long for that to be devoured
The table is cleared and the annual family competitions begin
It starts off with Blackjack
"The easy game for the weak" my grandpa claims
Then moves toward more complicated card games
Eventually we end with a fun game of Saboteur
My sister heads to bed after the last games
And the rest of my family goes to the living room to relax and catch up on events in each other's lives
I look into the twinkling eyes of everyone
And know they are having the best time right now
In the moment
Caught up in stories, silly opinions, and bountiful jumbles of laughter

snow night on the dead end
Meridith Carter Frazee

All was superabundant green
glowing and shadowed
All riverstench, silt and fish
sunhot oregano and sun beating brick.
reduced to contrast-
black and white and DayQuil-colored light flooding from the development
   across the river

my brother is throwing snowballs.
His arm jerks,
the ice glitters into a lamplit crescendo
the lump of snow disappearing into soft icy flakes before it even lands.
it is like watching a movie
in which the action remains constant,
faraway and fixed and
from below I study the tableau of cloud, parked truck, boy without gloves,
   snow shining and
myriad under the streetlight's glaring sunset.

neither day nor night
here, only weird and diffuse twilight
in which everything unseen is buried
and everything buried is quiet.

snow nights are the least constant of all seasons.
snow nights are the time before waking that escapes all clocks
snow nights are the kind of surgery in which you play guitar while they
   operate so you don't lose
all that you love-
snow nights are
the unrecognizable
the thoughtless wish.

disharmonious
Eliza Sanusi

tell me that you are not naive enough to think that fireflies
match blurry step with your circadian rhythm
turn heads to face you like sunflowers
breathe tired tales of you while dancing in sweaters
of light and humidity and heat and honey
intermingled with nostalgia like summer's last peaches

tell me a tale of illumination and peaches
that will outlast the fleeting flight of fireflies
give me more than smiles and honeyed
phrases give me worth and teach me rhythm
like the beat of our chests against our sweaters
grow roots for us both grow more than just flowers

when i look at you i don't know why i expected flowers
to bloom or your cheeks to burst into smiles like peaches
like the weight of my presence is comforting like sweaters
like the thought of us could whisk away our troubles on the backs of fireflies
but raindrops lose color like we lost rhythm
and slowly any dreams we had diluted to honey

moving on is impossible when honey
memories stick impetuously to flowers
destroying ripples and flows of smooth oceans and the rhythm
of patience in the springtime like peaches
and i lose hope that i will ever not find you in fireflies
aftershave and the strings i pulled spasmodically from your sweater
i thought happiness came in polaroids and blankets and sweaters

i thought happiness was when you first called me honey
i believed you when you told me it was fireflies
and midsummer's humid dreams and flowers
you forgot to mention the scent of half rotten peaches
and betrayal that permeated our rhythm

your knuckles beat slow with the boorish tap of rhythm
against my door pressed hard against my sweater
spastic tears and i lock eyes with the painting on the wall i see peaches
and pastels mixed in summer's prettiest shades and honey
dripping lazily from every flower
but then you leave with the fleetingness of fireflies

we spent our days chasing fireflies instead of dreams and rhythm
but the flowers' petals are temporary like perfume steeped in sweaters
maybe now you'll believe me that peaches are nothing more than mold
   dipped in honey.

Clean Cut
Ava Martin

Summer sun
Blistering heat
Yellow cushion plastered to sweaty legs
Water bottle riding shotgun
Gearshift to the left

Immersed in calm
The centripetal movement of the blades
Sleeves rolled up
Throttle imprisoned by fist
The steady murmur of the engine following behind

Same track on repeat
Row after Row
House above
River below
Out with the old
In with the new

A blur of green surrounding
Blade on blade
One will stand
Millions will fall

Tufts of grass caress wheels
Propelled by spinning gears
Drenched in sweat
Coated in dust

Gnats following
Mice fleeing
Day coming to a close
A job well done.

Lullaby
Tina Feng

I melt into your heavenly charm
My little creature
My blessing

One blink
your smile, like a blooming daisy,
gently sings the story of our love

Another blink
your wrinkled eyes like facets of a sparkling diamond
lightens up the fullness of my heart

Your breath
delicate and pure
blows kisses like the summer breeze
Against my cheek

Inhaling,
your heart tightly pounding next to mine
Crescendo then Decrescendo
fluctuating and exciting

Exhaling,
your newborn breath slows down
cradling you tightly in my arms,
tenderly humming the melodious song
safe and sound

Virginia I'll Miss You
Dawson Dickerson

My favorite view from my home
Are the Blue Ridge Mountains
The sun setting behind them
The farm across the street
And the horses galloping across the land.
The view gets better
Under winter's snow.

Another farm, not far away,
Was a playground for me and friend
Racing in a gator around a made up track
Once the daylight was gone we head inside
To a fresh-out-of-the-oven pizza and some soda
We played video games until the midnight air came
Then it was back outside to playing basketball under a spot light
Until the bugs swarmed us forcing us to go inside

These are things I will never forget
They are what made my childhood so great and unforgetful
Virginia I will miss you.

Nuclear
Mary Dwyer

Your voice was smoldering.
It filled the room
suffocating me suffocating
all of us
loved you we loved you deeper
as you struck the match and watched
my cotton, candy insides
melt
and vanish.

The sun kissed the horizon
and your cement filled songs
settled delicately
on top of my chest,
pinning my frozen soul
to the sand as I look out
into the waves and scream
for spring to
return.

Hidden Gravel Roads
Madilyn Glaser

On a late November morning, I drove through a fairly affluent neighborhood scanning the house numbers for the correct address. The apparent wealth of the neighborhood surprised me given the usual areas I delivered to as a Meals on Wheels volunteer. When I thought I was lost, however, the paved road ended, and the gravel road led me to Mr. King's home.

At that moment, I entered a new world. Three mobile homes sat beside each other in a secluded, wooded area. The overgrowth of vegetation indicated the structures' ages, but the neatness of one yard demonstrated great care. The trailer sat in this manicured, well-kept patch of land.

"Good morning, Mr. King!" I said.

With a smile brighter than any I had seen that day, he greeted me back. "Good morning, young lady! How are you?"

After handing him his meals, he made it clear that he wanted to talk, and I happily obliged. In his late seventies, he clearly struggled with his health and mobility, but this did not dampen his spirits. He burst with pride when describing his garden, the hours of effort he invested in it, and the sense of accomplishment he gained from pulling weeds.

"Do you see that tree over there? I planted it twenty years ago and watched it grow from a tiny seed." He gushed over his trees, shrubs, and vegetable garden as if they were his children or friends. Given how eager he was to talk to me, a complete stranger, perhaps they did serve as his friends.

As we chatted, he began to tell me about his family, the decades he lived in the trailer, and his beloved dogs. At one point, he began to discuss his employment.

"I do my best to work, but my health keeps me from doing as much as I would like," he said with sadness in his eyes. "People don't seem to understand that. They assume that because I get free meals or government money that I'm just lazy."

I attempted to comfort him, but my few words could do little to untangle years of discrimination. After talking about his life for almost an hour, I left with a greater understanding of and compassion for his situation.

My conversation with Mr. King also gave me a more profound understanding of people's experiences with financial insecurity. Seated on his porch, Mr. King began to discuss the difficulties of having an unstable employment.

He asked, "Do I buy my child's school books, or do I pay the electricity bill? What do I do about groceries when I have to pay for a hospital visit? How can I possibly choose between these?"

I had no answer for him. This question confronted me with a reality so different from my own stable economic situation. I thought of my home, the meal that would be waiting for me when I returned, the spacious environment in which I lived, all in comparison with the deeper layers of other humans' problems. I knew that the lessons I learned from Mr. King in those moments would be lessons I would carry with me throughout my life.

"Well, young lady, I can't say how much I appreciate you bringing me these delicious meals." He waved a wrinkled hand in my direction, and we both shared a smile. Before meeting him, I did not possess such a nuanced understanding of the program and its recipients.

Speaking to people from a place different from mine taught me the greater struggle of food insecurity. I now think more critically about government assistance programs and the many circumstances in which people may require them.

I see the flaws in the system, and the fact that people like Mr. King cannot meet their basic needs horrifies me. I one day aspire to work one-on-one with disadvantaged people to connect them to resources based on their specific situations, rather than assign a blanket solution to all people of the same socioeconomic class.

Moving forward in life, I hope to spend more time learning from these gravel roads hidden from sight due to social injustice, and nothing has changed.

To My Yellow Mimi

Ela Singleton

The soft yellow blanket drapes over my head concealing me from the world.
I walk aimlessly towards my father, peeking through the small holes,
Small ooos escape my mouth mimicking a ghost's cries.
My parents smile and laugh, acting as if they can't see me,
Entertaining my imagination.

I loved my Yellow Mimi down to scraps.
By the time I was 10 she was a pile of torn, fabric shreds.
I wasn't ready to let go,
I gave her a new home inside a handmade pink fabric bag held together by
   a safety pin.
When I was 13 the pink had become a faint nude color.

The amount of tears, laughs, and smiles shared with her mattered too much,
Leaving her behind wasn't an option.
She is part of me and letting go of her would make me incomplete.
Though she has holes, she always keeps me warm,
And her soft, faded yellow never seemed so bright.

Big Goofy Smile
Son Kim

Time is endless, what is in the past can never change, it will always be there as a form of memory, it might be forgotten, but no matter what, someonewill remember it had happened.

As a child growing up, I had many people surrounding me. Giving me unconditional love, giving me the support that I need in order to keep going and encourage me to try my best. In my whole family, I was the first child to be born that did not have to go through hardships when I was small. I had everything that I want, I did not have to go and work at a young age, I get to study in an international school, but most importantly, I have a family that loves me. At a young age, I did not understand what I had and I tend to believe that everyone have the same life as me. At the time, I had a friend that lived in the countryside part of the city, where my mom and aunt had grown up. As a kid, they would bring me back quite often and every time, I would always hang out with that one kid. He was the happiest go-lucky person I have ever met and his attitude never changed, he always have this big smile on his face and whenever he smile, we can see his missing tooth. He was always positive and nothing really let him down. When we first met, we were only seven year old and that friendship only lasted until I turn eleven.

Those four years were the most memorable year of my life. I did not have to worry too much about school, I did not have to think what I need to do in the future, I can stay focus as a kid. I would look forward to coming back to the countryside and hang out with the my friend and see what kind of adventure it will lead us to. I always had fun whenever I hang out with him and life never seems to be dull. However, during the beginning of the fifth year, due to an event that I can not seem to recall, it made me and him change. Thinking back, I was blind not being able to see what was coming, but I was small and was immature. When I came back, he greeted me as usual, with his big goofy smile waving at me. However, that smile was not genuine. He is smiling, but from hanging out with him a lot before I was able to recognize that the smile was not real. Something had happened and I was curious. I tried to ignore it and act like I did not notice anything, but as time goes by during the day, it becomes clearer and clearer. At the end of the day, after our usual adventure with the other kids in the village, I would brought it up. He looked at me in shock and said that he doesn't know what I'm talking about. It made me frustrated and to be frank, really angry because as a friend for quite some time, I would like to know what had happened since I wanted to help. He was quite persistent saying that nothing was wrong and after a while, I gave up trying to ask. My anger was at peak and I did not wanted to continue the conversation after that.

After that talk, I never really think about him again. I was childish, since I always thought that everything would revolve around me. I had trouble before, but nothing major really comes up. I was childish and partly an idiot for not trying to force it out of him and resulting in me avoiding him. Time went on and I had not met him since. Around three or four months later, my family forced me to go back despite my protest. When I arrive, no one was there to greet me and even though I was angry at that point, I did not really care. The day kept going and my frustration was getting the better of me. In the end, I asked my grandma where he is and she sighed. I did not know what had happened and rushed her to say but when she said it, I stood there, paralyzed by what she said. My friend, he jumped down the river two months earlier. Apparently, he was abused by his parents and they did not really care about him either. I spent that night crying and thinking what had gone wrong. What could I have done better and why was I so childish. I did not understand since he always looked happy and cheerful, I did not wanted to accept the fact that he was gone just like that and it made me hate myself for my actions.

Time is irreversible, what had been done cannot be undone, it will stay as a form of memory and it will never go away. Due to my childishness, I lost a life long friend and I regretted every single decision that I made, I regretted that I could not help him and I hated myself for not learning about the truth sooner. I still remember him, vivid in my mind, I was always envious of him and looked up to him. He may not be here anymore, but I know that I will never forget about him and his big, goofy smile.

Tobias

Tylar Schmitt

The bell rang and Ms. Butterfield wrote three words on the chalkboard. She underlined them too.

Show and Tell.

In the middle of the class, Pippa Pickle sat at her desk with a colossal gray cage on top.

Inside perched a blue and yellow macaw. She patted the top of its head and fed it Fruit Loops.

"Shut up," it said.

"Is that a bird?" asked J.T. Hudson, who was sitting to her right.

"No. It's a macaw," explained Pippa. "His name is Tobias and he's my Granddaddy's.

What did you bring?"

"Dirt."

"I brought my coin collection," said Madison Monroe, who was sitting to Pippa's left. "I even have one from Canada."

"Shut up," Tobias said.

"Alright class," began Ms. Butterfield. "Who would like to go first?"

Everyone's hands shot up like cannons. "Me! Me! Me! Me!"

"Not everyone at once. Let me see…" She scanned the room with her beady eyes and her wrinkled finger. "How about J.T.?"

"Oh yeah!" He jumped up from his chair and ran to the front. "So, I brought dirt. Dirt lives in the ground…"

Pippa paid no attention. She continued to pat Tobias's head and feed him Fruit Loops. "I like the purple ones the best," she whispered to him. "But Grandaddy says they all taste the same."

"Shut up," Tobias said.

"Why does your bird say shut up?" asked Madison.

"He's a macaw. And macaws copy things they hear."

"Do you say shut up a lot?"

"No." Pippa popped another Fruit Loop in Tobias's mouth. "But my Grandaddy does."

"Shut up," Tobias said.

Madison scoffed. "Does he say anything else?"

"Sometimes he says shi-"

"So, in conclusion, dirt rocks." J.T. said. Applause engulfed him as he walked back to his desk.

"Who's up next?" asked Ms. Butterfield.

The canons shot again. "Me! Me! Me! Me!"

"How about…Madison?"

Everyone groaned. Madison grabbed her coin collection and strutted to the front. "For show and tell, I brought my coin collection. This one is from Canada…"

"Shut up," Tobias said.

J.T turned to Pippa. "Can I have a Fruit Loop?"

"No. They're for Tobias."

"What about bird food?"

"My Grandaddy didn't buy any."

"Shut up," Tobias said.

J.T.'s eyes grew wide. "Whoa, he talks!"

"Duh. All macaws do."

"Does he fly?"

"He has wings."

"But does he fly?"

"My Granddaddy doesn't let him out of the cage." Pippa fed Tobias the last Fruit Loop. It was purple.

"What you should take away from my presentation is that my coin collection is the best." Madison concluded. There was scattered applause as she sat back down at her desk.

"Alright." Ms. Butterfield pushed her glasses up her nose. "Pippa?"

Pippa heaved the cage off her desk and slammed it onto the floor with a thud. Tobias didn't flinch. She pushed the cage up to the front of the room with the force of a fawn and stopped when it reached the corner of Ms. Butterfield's desk.

"Can you help me lift it?" she asked.

Ms. Butterfield sighed and lifted Tobias onto her desk. "That's one ugly bird," she said.

Pippa thanked her for her help and stood tall. "I brought my Grandaddy's blue and yellow macaw. His name is Tobias and he has a green stripe on top of his head. One fact about Tobias is that he says shut up a lot."

"Shut up," Tobias said. Everyone giggled.

Pippa looked at Tobias, standing there in his colossal cage. She noticed the black and white stripes that laid across his eyes, and then noticed the red ones that laid across his feathers. They were uneven: long and short and deep and shallow. She knew that macaws weren't supposed to have red stripes at all. There were only supposed to be blue and yellow.

"Another fact about Tobias is that he doesn't fly. Even though most macaws do." She looked at Tobias one more time. "Until now."

She opened the latch of the cage. At first, Tobias didn't know what to do. He just sat there, said "shut up." But then he twitched his head back and forth and observed the openness of the classroom around him. He spread his wings, jumped out of the cage, and started to fly around.

"PIPPA!" Ms. Butterfield shrieked.

Tobias's wings spread like fresh paint on the ceiling of the classroom. He flew from corner to corner, yelling "Shut up! Shut up!" He cawed at his freedom.

Ms. Butterfield grabbed a meter stick. "Come here, ugly bird!" She chased him as he flew; Pippa and her classmates cackled. Ms. Butterfield plunged her meter stick up in the air, aiming at Tobias's stomach, and missed it by a centimeter. Then he pooped right on top of her head. It was a Fruit Loop smoothie, and it dripped all the way down her back to the toes of her bony feet.

"Hahaha, Pippa's bird pooped on Ms. Butterfield's head!" J.T screamed. Everyone became hyenas.

"That. Is. IT!" Ms. Butterfield gripped her meter stick like a baseball bat and charged right at Tobias. She swung at him, hit his back, and he fell straight to the floor. Blood splattered on the white tile.

"NO!" Pippa ran to the back of the class. Everyone followed her.

"I don't know who you think you are, Pippa Pickle, setting a macaw loose in my classroom and allowing it, allowing it, allowing it to- I'm calling the principal!" Ms. Butterfield dialed the phone. "Hello, Principal Wagner. I must report that I just killed a bird in my classroom, but it was self defense, and it was Pippa Pickle's..."

Pippa held Tobias in her lap. He laid absolutely still. She didn't care that his blood was getting all over her baby blue pants.

"Is he dead?" asked J.T, leader of the pack above her.

She patted the top of Tobias's head. "Yeah."

Growing Up
Maddie Kwasnick

Do you remember the years of color?
When the world was a blue and green floor rug
Circled by lively Kindergarteners.
When you waited for your turn on the playground swing,
Because you wanted so badly to be able to fly.
Your primary school was decorated with primary colors,
And you were taught that sharing was caring.
 If only it had stuck.

What about the middle years?
When the world finally started to become conceivable.
When you started to wonder what he thought, what she thought,
And what life was all about.
Your parents could help you solve any math problem,
And you thought you could plan your life
By choosing a vocation based solely on your favorite class.
If only you planned to be happy.

Do you remember the years of confusion?
When you finally noticed evil hiding
In every shadowed corner of a much-too-real world.
When your parents confessed that they had long since forgotten
How to do trigonometry.
You were told to plan your life,
As if it were an assignment that you would turn in to God
When you stepped through those pearly gates with high hopes of at least a B+.
It was all about you, wasn't it?

Now you've reached the years of black and white, wrong and right.
When the world is broken,
And you have to decide whether you try to fix it or not.
When you wonder why you're even here.
The toxic selfishness leaks into your heart,
And you only allow it because you're oblivious.
You've strayed far from the roadmap of life
That you created in those years of confusion.
Everything is clear now; various truths are laid before you
On a platter that you get to select from.
You were told that growing up would only make life better,
But in the end, you still wish you could fly.

Ode to the Internet

Hewson Duffy

1.
The monsters under our beds
Shift uneasily on creaking floorboards,
Shielding their eyes from our shining nightlights.

We just lie there, you and I,
Our lowered blinds blocking out the sky,
Sticking fingers in our ears
As if it will drown out the monsters' murmur,
Or restlessly tapping the algorithmic looking glass
As if it won't hollow us.

0.
This time, the forty-day flood isn't of water,
But of pixels. The angry clouds spew not raindrops,
But harsh blue pinpricks in a relentless torrent.
They hit the ground—one click, then another,
Then a billion (louder than buzzing static)—
Becoming a river as massive as the Amazon:
Terabytes high, gigahertz fast,
Scrolling through cities, submerging them.

This time, we sinners don't drown but choke
One by zero by one, individuality suffocating
Under the endless current.

1.
We've become afraid of the silence
Instead of the dark, afraid of the time at night
When the day's empty chatter ceases
And our thoughts—grimy and pockmarked,
Their misshapen mouths full of crooked teeth—
Crawl out of their hiding places, the time when
The only monsters under our beds are ourselves.

Cyclicality
Charlotte Walters

With dusk emerges fireflies,
miniscule wings beating to the rhythm
of the clock, counting until twilight flowers
into darkness, sweatered
in thick humidity that drips like honey
from tender peaches.

There was nothing sweeter than peaches,
the illumination of fireflies
unfathomable through honey
soaked eyes, seeing only the rhythm
of sunshine, not the timeline of the sunset, my sweater
of warmth and blooming flowers.

Eyes turned to the sky, I was a sunflower
oblivious of the fingerprint bruises on peaches
and the thorns that snagged my sweater.
I saw only permanence in the glow of fireflies,
not mere placeholders for stars in the rhythm
of nightfall that seeps into dusk like honey.
I painted my skin with honey,

plucking petals from the garden's flowers
until I heard the audible rhythm
of the clock, so when peaches
rotted and a chill stole the fireflies
I despised my thorn ripped sweater.
I watched as time withered my sweater

and the crust of honey
on my skin floated away like fireflies
as I searched for permeable permanence in the flowers
and stuffed cans with peaches
to slow the cruel rhythm.

I decided to make my own rhythm,
swaddled in a time dampened sweater
to grasp memories instead of peaches
with desperate hands, because flowers
can't grow without seasons and darkness can't be prevented by fireflies.

So I let fireflies weave their own rhythm
and flowers bloom in the holes of my sweater
because I can find the sweetness of honey without peaches.

see, i told you i loved you.
Maya Goldstein

see: 1. to perceive by the eye: i like to think i *see* you for you. i enjoy *seeing* the dimples under your eyes in a genuine smile. i *see* your hands and long fingers and think of the many times they held me. i *see* how you *see* her, the way you used to *see* me. 2. to come to know: i have *seen* you as a replacement for where my bad thoughts take me. i *see* you as my beacon of light. the wide arms of your grandparents, the quick nod of understanding before i finish speaking, the tickling under my chin. 3. to be the setting or time of: you have *seen* all of me in the last few months. you have *seen* my tears, dysfunctional family, beautiful friends. you have taken note of all that's been endured and stuck around just long enough for me to get comfortable. i like to imagine us stuck in the wrong time period. it gives me hope that this is not the end. 4. to take care of; provide for: i will *see* to it that i love you until the end. i tried to *see* that you were better than you thought you could be, but i failed. i wanted to *see* that you were okay, and i died trying. 5. to find acceptable or attractive: "i don't know what you *see* in him," they would say. i don't know what you didn't *see* in yourself. i *saw*, past tense, your kindness and humility, your ability to move on quickly; something i would learn to hate. i *saw* your eyes light up at the thought of someone *seeing* something in you that you never *saw*. i *saw* your hands jitter when i first grabbed them and how they'd start to sweat if i held them for too long. i *saw* your way of caring for those you loved. i *saw* the way you always found something to love in other people but never yourself. 6. to acknowledge or consider something being pointed out: *see*, i told you i loved you. but after you said it first. *see*, i told you i wanted this. but after it was too late. *see*, i told you you would mess this up. but only you said that.

The Beauty in Everything
Lindsay King

Takashi had always said he was observant.

"Isaac," he would say in his sweet tenor, "you have a knack for finding the beauty in everyone and everything."

Or, when he was pissed off, he would say, "Isaac, how is it that you have the time and energy to put into noticing random shit no one else cares about?" He would always feel bad afterwards, but he kept saying it, because it was true, and Isaac could admit it. The thing is, he had never actually had anyone to rant to about actual shit he was going through, until he met Takashi. After that, he wasn't going through shit anymore, because he felt like a king around him. Somehow, the nervousness, jitters, the anxiety and depression that kept him awake at night and haunted him during the day simply melted away as he stared into Takashi's caramel eyes. It wasn't that his life before had been horrible. He was a teacher at an elite academy. His students liked him. He got a decent paycheck. He had a few friends. That's about all. Looking back, his life could only be described in short, mundane sentences, because nothing really happened, he just sort of . . . existed. But that all changed when he met Takashi. They hit it off immediately, despite Isaac's in vain attempt not to stutter or say anything stupid to his colleague.

"See, Takashi, how beautiful this maple is? Its leaves are almost crimson near the stem, but here they're green . . ."

"Isaac, you have a knack for finding the beauty in everyone and everything." Isaac rolled his eyes at this, having heard his little speech a thousand and one times, but this time Takashi continued.

"That must have been why you took a chance on me, a bitter, hardcore son of an admiral."

"I took a chance on you because I saw kindness in your eyes, Takashi. And our boss made me," he said, watching a smile spread across his boyfriend's face.

"I'm glad he did."

"Me too."

Takashi took Isaac into his strong arms, pulling him into a tight hug. He felt his chin rest on Isaac's head.

"Isaac," Takashi said without moving.

"Mmhmm?"

"Were you using my shampoo?"

With a sob, Isaac is yanked back to the present. He runs his fingers over the newly carved gravestone. The fresh red clay clings to his palms and knees. He lays back onto the dirt and looks into the sky. He watches as the sun filters through the crimson and green leaves, sunspots dancing around above, as he cries. *Nothing should be beautiful. The beauty of the world is gone.* He wraps his arms around himself.

Isaac, you have a knack for finding the beauty in everyone and everything.

The Room
Youjia Yang

    At least, I can call it home. In the afternoons, soft light comes through the half-visible drapes, spanning across the living room. They're only the first barrier of concealment one uses against the outside. Of course, there exists another layer of full-on thick curtains. The curtains were beautifully woven designer products… 10 years ago. But the ends were gray with dirt and use, touching the floor once in a while. A leather couch bought from… what's their name? Right, Givenchy. There was a little hole on the seat, patched together by band-aids. But that's fine, plenty of cushions of every texture and style covered the hole. The thread hanging out from once pristine edges caressed the damaged leather. Chandeliers, crystal-covered lamps lit the room. Though one light bulb, actually no two, its shape mimicking the shape of flames, doesn't work anymore… It doesn't matter… Covered in a thin layer of dust, it's barely noticeable. The coffee table had a globe in the center. It was said to be very expensive…. Scratches, pen marks covered the table surface. There was once a boat. Now it lies half stuck amongst lily pads. Its hollows serve as a home for families of frogs. At least they have a place for home. Protected from light. The optimal condition for rotting. Nothing new has been bought or might I say, given, in 5? no, at least 6 years. He, my Dad, used to buy wood, pieces of wood. Carry it in to burn in the just breathtaking marble fireplace. It's been a cold 4 years. On the mantelpiece, two calligraphy brushes hang from a structure intended to hold eight. Their fur ends feathered out, disorderly. Eight, lucky number eight. 88836, his license number. The sound of wheels, the sound of a car door slamming. No one acknowledged this. Heads down…eat. Though occasionally, just occasionally interrupted with a sideways glance, a light reflecting off the pupils. This voice again, in the same tone, "You know what to say, don't say anything about…" she always pushed out a little laugh. A lighthearted tone, an indication of normality. No knocks, he only struts. Those distinct footsteps.

Speaking with authority or, power?… Pride…The same old way he called me, he called my sister's name. He came to play with her. Her eyes glistened, her mouth curved up. She told him her stories, kindergarten, toys, leaning forward. He listened. Leaning back, pulling out his phone, checking something. Two possible choices, money or sex. With an occasional nod, a sound of agreement, their 'conversation" continued. "There are no parents in this world that don't love their kids…" Someone or something…said those words. I wonder if this is possible. Do I want his love? Is it a normal thing that a child wishes for a parent's love. Why do I not feel… Is it still possible, for a father to love a daughter? Is there a chance that he still does. Is he from heaven or from hell? Please, please, please, someone, someone tell me.

Father
Nola Ralls

You have a collect call from Walter Ralls an inmate at Albemarle Regional Jail, a Virginia State Correctional Facility. To accept the charges for this call press 3. If you do not wish to pay for this call please hang up. If you no longer wish to accept calls from a correctional facility press star. Your call is being transferred. Thank you for using MCI.

Warmth
Robin Guziejka

I knew it would be coming soon. Maybe it was Hermes, or maybe it was the Reaper. Maybe it was nothing. Well, not nothing, because it was definitely something. It was harder to suck in enough air to stay awake and talk to my visitors. If you don't stay awake, you won't eat, and then the process just comes faster. I had tubes all around me. In my veins, in my nose, and in places I'd rather them not be. I rub my swollen knuckles and I'm almost instantly met with purple splotches all around. I feel myself getting weaker everyday. There isn't a day that goes by when I don't cry. I cry for things I never thought about before. Perhaps it was because I was so selfish in my earlier years. Or maybe I wasn't, and I tried too hard which gave me all my regrets. I could have done better, I could have forgave and apologized more. I wish I could have stopped myself from yelling, and I would never raise my hand to a soul. I think of all the people I must have hurt, and the tears sting more and more each time I remember my cruelty. They sting like the needles in my hands, but they don't fall out and spill my blood on the floor like they do. I like to think that all the pain I feel now is torture for all my wrongdoings. That must be what it is, shouldn't it? If I was nicer, maybe I could have just fallen asleep and drifted off into the universe, never knowing. That's how I always dreamt it would be. I would watch my children grow up and have children, but that's a pipedream. I could have done better. I would go to more baseball games and I would hug them more, maybe they would come around if I had. I'll always remember what my Nona told me. You should never hate someone, you're too pretty to hate. Which was translated into the classic, "Treat others how you would want to be treated." If I loved more, they would love me too. My face is wet, but my arms are so sore I can't lift them to my face. I sit in my sorrow, and I allow all my demons to devour me. They rip and tear, and leave me bare for all the world to see. But a light comes into view. And they are warm, and excellent, and all the things I never knew. It washed away all the bad, and cleansed my soul. They placed their hands at my limbs, and I couldn't help but be met with the feeling of absolute bliss. It was inviting, and it told me it would be okay. I wish I could see, and absorb its full excellence, but I haven't been able to make out features for a while. But I knew this love. It was the love and safety you felt as a child when your mother held you when you saw monsters in the dark or when you scraped your knee and you were sure you'd have to amputate that leg.. I didn't think I had any lately, but I was wrong. My mind was the monsters, and life was the pavement I smacked my body on so often. I wish it didn't take all my life to figure that out. For once, I was breathing clearer than I ever had before and my cheeks grew to meet my eyes. I was okay.

A father
Ari Pyle

His heart felt as if it broke in half as he did
His daughter's smile lit up his world
His daughter's smile encouraged him to be better
His daughter's smile was always there
Except when it wasn't
Her smile was missing
Her face was blank
It was immovable
It was horrid
And everytime he stared at it
It filled him with disgust
He hated it
So that's why
That's why
He had to
He stared at his daughter's face again,
Her face was contorted in fear,
And his heart felt as if it broke in half as he did

Amaya Rose
LaShalle Schornberg

i never held you. i stared at your body. purple. kissed with decay. never cradled you. i didn't dare hold your hand or play with your toes. your feet too big for your body, or at least that's what i was told. runner, they said. clumsy, they said. the future of hope turned grim. endless possibilities of who you were and what you could become cloud my vision. i'll never know. you rest so soundlessly in the unforgiving january ground. cold. the world is cold without you. a life once so warm cut as simply as a string. stolen. taken. too soon. you're in a place without pain and i should be thankful. selfish. i am selfish for wanting to have time with you. you would have struggled. cried. hurt. bled. but somehow, i convince myself, that would be better. to tell you how much i love you would outshine the horrors of this world. i can't hold you. i can't see you. i can't talk to you. yet i say: "I love you, Amaya Rose"

But You Didn't
Nora Li

When I was two,
I pulled your hair hard,
as if yanking grass from soil.
The twinge made your face contort,
looking at your grimace,
I started laughing...
You rubbed your head to release the pain.
I thought you would scream at me,
...but you didn't.
You pinched my nose and kissed my forehead,
"What a naughty girl."
You looked into my eyes
with eyes full of unconditional love.
When I was four,
I indulged in painting.
After spoiling all the paper,
I reached my mischievous little hands up to your new white shirt,
then, I showed you my masterpiece, proudly,
and awaited your praise.
Your laugh faded away.
I took a step back and dropped my head down.
My heart beat rapidly.
I thought that you would spank me hard and
kick me out of your room,
but you didn't.
You sighed head shaking.
You stepped towards me.
I closed my eyes, waiting for the pain of your slap,
but you just tousled my hair and

wiped off my tears gently.
I sank into your embrace and
buried my face into your neck
like a peevish cat.
When I was six,
I asked for money to buy a textbook,
but I spent all the money on stickers and postcards.
That was the first time I lied to you.
You found the cards when you cleaned up the room.
You threw those stickers down in front of me
and questioned me.
I saw the disappointment in your eyes.
I saw the anguish in your eyes.
A clenching sensation imprisoned my stomach.
A screeching shame filled my body.
My eyes grew sore.

No ocean could compete
with my tears of regret.
You hate me--
I know it.
Say it.
...but you didn't.
You pulled me closer to you,
and told me, in a low but sincere voice,
"Remember. You never need to lie to me."
When I was eight
I got the highest score in my math class
holding my test above my head,
I rushed out of the classroom.,
I wanted to share my happiness with you.
I had no doubt,

you would pick me up,
spin me around and
kiss my cheek.
....but you didn't.
I saw you on the street with a strange woman.
You hugged her and kissed her instead,
just as you kissed Mom in the past.
You put another boy on your back,
just where you put me in the past.
I wished for you to tell me "It's not true!"
I wanted you to tell me "It's a nightmare."
...but you didn't.
Instead, you had a quarrel with Mom.
I heard the sound of glass crashing on the floor.
I heard the sound of my heart break, as
the fragments scattered across the floor.
I heard a heavy door slam.
I heard Mom sobbing.
I thought you would come back
the next day,
grasp me in your embrace
and kiss my face.
But you didn't.
Mom opened the door of my room;
I saw the tears in her eyes.
Hugging me, she said "From now on
it's just the two of us...."
I was a wooden statue in her arms.
I didn't believe her.
I was sure you would return--

But you didn't.

The Fire

Aaron Osborne

 The darkness of my room was ultimate - no light could seep through my scrunched eyelids. My head was wedged in the space between my mattress and my headboard, in a awkward, angled sort of way. One pillow lay perpendicular, above my neck, assisting in constructing my own isolated world. My other pillow was grasped tightly against my side, tethering me to reality, and my blanket veiled me from that world. Muffled cries and piercing words found their way to my ears.

 Against all instincts, I allowed my blanket to slide to the floor as I turned my head upwards. From the hall outside my bedroom, a burning light seeped into the previously unbroken darkness. Only my mother was visible through the doorway. Her grayish-brown hair shimmered in the dull, yellow light, with each strand reflecting into my eyes. She had on white, muddied running shoes - each instance she brought her foot down onto the carpet sent a rattling through the floor. Her unbroken gaze was locked on an unseen figure down the hall. Like a bull preparing to charge, my brother would respond in the same manner. A symphony of stomps and a dissonance of shouts fueled by unrelenting anger resonated through the house. Pictures of smiling faces - remnants of a life long forgotten - trembled on the wall. Melancholy and frustration had made company in all of our minds, refusing to depart from their new home; our photographed trips provided only a fleeting respite, and each stomp skewed that reality even farther away. Fingers lunged forward in accusation, fists were pumped in anger. The two became equals on this battlefield. It was not a mother disciplining a child, rather it was two people attempting to communicate years of seething discontent in the only way they knew how.

 I retreated to the embracing comfort of my blanket, sweeping it off the floor and over my eight-year-old head. The salty taste of tears had become a comfort, and I indulged this thirst. At another stomp, my eyes were ripped open. I became adjusted to the encompassing darkness - I could so clearly see the long forgotten items that hid under my bed: an empty water bottle, a toy

plane, a box of art supplies, a framed picture. A fictional reality unfolded in my mind. In a disagreement of two, a third is the only resolution. I became the hero in this reality, the one to end the fighting - if only for tonight.

My reality intertwined with the world. I began to attempt to realize the fictional events I had imagined. The first step was the easiest. I allowed my feet to dangle above the carpet as my eyes remained fixed on the source of the musical harmony. Pushing myself from the comfort of my bed, my legs trembled in the effort to keep my body aloft. The carpet beneath me provided my feet some semblance of warmth in the cold, dark house. As my willpower began to accrue, I was drawn closer to the fiery luminance bleeding in from the hall. I took a moment to regard my room - as if it was the last I would see it. The reflection in my mirror was not my own - it was that of a confused, lost boy. I was not lost, I was not confused. Forgetting this, my valor reached its precipice; I would step out into the hall now or I would return to my own deaf, dark world.

My feet, of their own volition, carried me the rest of the way through the door. In the briefest second before I spoke, neither member of my family acknowledged me, so locked in their own battle. I stood as a spectator, only a foot away from each of their tear-stained faces. The original subject of the argument, long forgotten amidst the screams, no longer mattered.

"Stop it!" my crackling, prepubescent voice cried out as loud as my lungs could muster. Hearing myself, I realized the intended loud, captivating shout had come out more as a yelp from a dying animal. The two enemies, in that moment, united. With their attention briefly redirected, they each unleashed their frustration towards me, condemning me to the confines of my room.

"Go to bed!" was the only response my mom offered.

"Stay out of it!" my brother screeched, joining in.

Fear built up like plaque as my reality crumbled down. It muddied my mind and filled my throat. My mouth opened as if I was going to speak, but I never did. My jaw locked, my nose ran with accumulated mucus, and my wet, puffy eyes made the dim light of the hall appear in brilliant, flaming ribbons. Those eyes searched for sympathy or compassion in either of their faces, darting back and forth between the two warriors. I closed my mouth closed to swallow, and

it did not reopen to respond. I was again a spectator. I did not contemplate a side to join, a fighter to bet on. Instead, I swiveled on my naked heels, as the fire behind me singed my skin.

 The stomping and accusation reignited as if it were never extinguished. I made the trek through the darkness back to my bed. The floor continued to shake and walls continued to echo the clamor. Walking past the mirror, I saw my own reflection and the night surrounding me. My reflection was defeated and isolated, drowning in the murky darkness. The fire I failed to muffle would only leave burns by the morning, with each interaction risking to rekindle it. The draining process would repeat; the roaring wildfire could only ever be temporarily forgotten - never completely smothered. The reassuring presence of my bed comforted me, however. And I, again, retreated to the impenetrable darkness below my pillows. My head returned to its uncomfortable cranny as the rocking of the floor and the muffled cries carried me into a fragmented sleep.

Sanguine

Miriam Topchyan

She set the medicine bottle gently onto the table, the glass a dull brown dirtied with smudges of grey. The dark liquid settled, the pale yellow label torn and curling over on the sides— it was the most this shell of a town could offer.

Slowly taking a seat by the rickety hospital bed, she leaned over to brush her younger brother's disheveled hair out of his face. Darkening eye bags hung below his exhausted eyes, his skin deathly pale to near translucency, littered with long scars and protruding veins. From an early age, her ill brother would spend weeks on end cooped up in the hospital, alone in rooms of achromatic walls, the old paint cracking and peeling. Weeks would span to months, and months would span to years, until he eventually never left. As of late, he could barely even sit up straight on his own, instead opting to lie back against the slightly-propped up pillows. On each day of her visits, she would find him in the same position— a tattered book in his hands as he wistfully stared out the window, the streets outside harboring the occasional passerby. Today, she found him simply staring at his hands as they rested in his lap, eyes motionless as if frozen in a trance. Her heart ached to see her brother in such a painful state.

"Hey," she whispered, restraining the volume of her voice so as not to startle him, "I've got your medicine. They let me bring it up to you." His barely-focused eyes turned to face her, a semblance of a smile tugging at the corners of his lips despite himself. "You're back," he murmured, relief evident on his features, "you came back."

"Of course I'm back," she responded with a strained smile in return, handing his dose of the medication over into his hands. "How's your book going?"

"It's… interesting," he managed, his voice soft and slow. "I'm almost finished with it. The adventures in it… they're…" His face fell, a crestfallen sigh escaping him as he weakly reached for his book, fingers skimming across the torn cover. "They're better than anything I'll ever get to do."

"Don't say that," she frowned. "You're going to get better soon, you *know* that."

"I'm not." With a bitter, hollow laugh, his gaze met hers again. "I'm never

going to be able to get out of this room again, *you* know that." Before she could respond, he continued. "But it's not all so bad. After all, maybe once I'm gone—"

"Hey."

"Maybe once I'm gone, I'll be able to follow you on all sorts of adventures."

"*Hey*."

"I'll finally get to see the outside world again," he persisted, a hint of desperation in his voice. "Once I die—"

"*That's enough!*" she snapped. She hadn't realized that she'd jumped to her feet, her chair scraping loudly against the floor as it was sent backwards. He violently flinched at her raised voice and impulsive movements, eyes wide and staring at her in fear.

"…Sorry," he mumbled after a short pause, slumping back against the pillows, breaking eye contact to stare at the ceiling as his exhausted tone returned. His book lay forgotten at the foot of the bed. "Sorry. I shouldn't have brought it up. Forget I said anything…"

Her shoulders relaxed, sighing as her previous anger replaced itself with remorse. What was she thinking, raising her voice at her brother when he was already in such a poor state—

"Excuse me, Miss," came the subdued voice of a nurse as she entered the room, pacing up to the bed. "Your brother will be needing his rest, now."

Tearing her eyes from the hospital bed, shoving down her frustrated thoughts of *but I just got here,* she glanced up at her brother for a final time, whispering her sullen goodbyes before being sent out into the endless corridors. The walls were painted with a thin, chipped coat of a sickly, desaturated green, with the faults in the appearance covered with the contrast of bright paintings.

She paused at the nearest, allowing herself to lose herself for just a mere moment. Sliding her eyes shut, she envisioned her and her brother, surrounded by the same, flowering red-and-pink blossoms depicted in the paintings as they wandered the lands, wind caressing their skin and leading them to paths untrodden.

Alone in the dark halls, a sister silently prayed for her younger brother—prayed for his recovery, prayed for his health, prayed for the day they'd sit together under the stars.

A Letter From Hope

Sarah Swagerl

I cry to Hope
Why have you forsaken me
Why have you not saved me from this nightmare
Why are you deaf to my pleas
Why, as he lays in this cold building, do you not ease his pain
In this place where the light blinds the eyes
Filling rooms, the sick wither away praying for Hope to come and save them
Oxygen tanks line the halls breathing life into their weak bodies

I held his bare hand in the sun that seeped into the ICU
I knew he was waiting for the real sun
To walk outside, feel the breeze, smell the coming winter
Just one last time
But it became darker each day without the beautiful light,
The Hope of his world
He had felt pain before
The pain of withdrawal
The pain of betrayal
The pain of loss in all corners of his life
But never pain like this
A pain so inescapable it radiated like poison into his bones, blood, heart, and soul
Haunting his dreams, weeping like a newborn babe, begging
"My Hope, where is the love you promised to us
Why do you not carry me when I need you most"
It became harder to hold onto Hope as we walked down the dark path
Slowly losing sight of it, no longer able to follow

So we waited and waited as those around us slowly forgot the sorrow in our hearts and lives
School, work, hospital, homework, food, sleep, repeat…
It became normal as the days passed
No longer mattered to the people around us
We walk past those halls of praying families
They also understand the darkness that plagues our family
But in our hearts, there was a flicker of Hope
Calling to us from my father's bed

In the waiting room, it called my name
Walking down the hall, arms open wide
Whispering, Hope said to me
I am your refuge and fortress from the pestilence of this place
Do not fear the terrors of the night for I shine brighter than these dark days
I will rescue him on wings of healing
Be patient and do not fear for I will honor my promise of Hope to you

Hope continues to keep its promise
Slowly easing his hurt body,
Returning his once lost smile
I still see it sometimes at home
He shivers remembering when his soul was scared
Pain still plagues his body,
Healing slower than his mind
Forever marked by 51 days and nights in that room
But, in the deepest moments of loss and sorrow
Hope stands there waiting for me to hear its call
Waiting to be found
Waiting to be trusted
Because Hope only truly works when we are willing to follow it

Leading us on a new path full of new possibilities
Hope has a letter waiting for everyone
Waiting in the halls of your soul
For you to find in the moments of pain, despair, loss
And for all who find hope, strength shall be renewed

Last Conversation with Grandfather

Trent Moran

When the time comes where I will have to stand there beside my grandfather's' deathbed, god willing this will not be for a while, I do not think I would have enough time to get everything off my chest that I would like to. I will not forget the numerous amounts of lessons he had taught me even though half the time I did not think he knew what he was talking about, but if I was wrong, he was one hell of a smart guy.

We would probably talk about all the times on the farm where there was a piece of equipment or an old car that needed to be fixed and he would work on it while I stood there holding a flashlight having absolutely no idea what he was doing and listen to him say "gosh darn this bugger" everytime something did not work right. He must have done something right though because every single time he got it back up and running. I would thank him for teaching me how to shoot a gun and all the times I have sat in the freezing cold hoping to see an animal move.

There are so many things my grandfather had taught me over the years that I can not even keep track of them all, but in my eyes the most important thing he has taught me is work ethic. He wakes up every morning at 5am to start working on the farm; everything he does is focused solely on his farm. I have never seen anyone so passionate about one single thing than he is about his small farm. He has been someone I have looked up to over my life and he will keep inspiring me throughout my life. His advice to me would be to keep a positive attitude no matter what. He always told me "the one thing in the morning you can always change is your attitude," and I am sure that is exactly what he would say to me then.

I do not think I would ever be able to say goodbye to my grandfather. I do not think anyone would ever be able to say goodbye to someone who means that much to you. I think the only thing you can say is "see you soon" with a small bit of hope in your heart that somehow, some way that you will end up in the same place when you pass away.

Crash
Jenna DiGirolamo

Rush.
Sirens wailing, people crying, dizzy expressions
of victims waking from a place beyond reality.
Some, still sleeping, will never wake to say goodbye.

Crumpled bodies litter the scene.
The road is as covered by shattered glass as it is the rain, falling slowly.
"Fight. Hold on," they whisper. "Just a little longer."
They are speaking to lifeless faces.

I blink back the water that falls on my eyelashes.
How did this happen?
How did we get here?
Did I cause the accident?
Am I the reason for this chaos?
No.

I sit up gradually to absorb what lies in front of me.
A man, standing at the heart of the chaos, unscathed from
   the accident, covers his face with his
hands.
The rain is still falling, faster now.
"I thought I was fine. I only drank a little bit. Are they going to be okay?"
His question was not a question at all. He knew the answer.
Selfish.

How quickly things can change, like a bolt of lightning striking the sky.

It occurs instantly, profoundly, shockingly, unexpectedly.
No one can offer explanation as to why these things happen.
The rain stops. It cannot last forever.
One by one the victims are carried from the scene.

Blurry vision.
A voice tells me not to be afraid, not to be discouraged,
   for He is with me wherever I go.
Now the sun is shining, drying the tears on desperate faces
Restoring life among the lifeless. There's hope now, even healing.

But not just flowers need rain to grow.

Voices of the Dark
Stevie Tyree

The moon and the stars illuminated the dark and seemingly soulless night sky as Memphis lay on a tattered blanket situated on the sidewalk. It was always in the dead of night that he heard the most inexplicable noises. After the events of last year, his brain would often concoct situations that were not real, that were not of reality. He could not separate himself from his thoughts and from what was real. As he remained stationed on the cold and cratered concrete pavement, the bizarre noises that survived in his psyche grew louder. These noises warped his view of the world.

Memphis opened his eyes. He no longer lay on the cold sidewalk where he had fallen asleep the night before. He had awoken in a bedroom with 12 foot ceilings and enormous windows that provided views that overlooked the sprawling cityscape. Memphis rolled out of the king-sized bed and stumbled into the en suite bathroom. He looked at himself in the mirror and almost couldn't believe what stared back at him. He had gone from a homeless man wandering the streets at night in search of warmth and shelter to a man in a gold colored silk robe in a home that stretched an entire floor of a highrise. Memphis had been given a second chance.

Before the fall of his company, Memphis was one of the most influential business leaders in the region. He was an individual to be looked up to, someone that people aspired to be. That was until he was arrested on suspicion of tax evasion and he was forced to resign as chairman of his company and sell all of his assets. Everything that he had fought for, everything that he had dedicated his entire life to... was gone. Memphis only served two years in prison, but the ramifications of his actions would walk with him for the rest of his days. After his release, he resorted to drugs. It just seemed easy. He had never experienced anything so difficult, he had never felt so helpless, and he desperately needed something to numb reality.

He slowly crept away from the mirror and searched for any sign of a date or time. On his bedside table, he saw his phone. Memphis scurried to his

phone and turned it on. It was March 5th, the day of the FBI raid that was conducted on his home. It was too late to mend the pieces of his life back together. It was too late to change anything. It was too late to apologize to his family for the shame that he would bring them.

    The piercing rays of the sun peeked through the cracks between the towering buildings that surrounded Memphis. The voices that roamed through his head the night before had vanished, and reality had struck. He was still just a homeless man that lay on a tattered blanket spread across the sidewalk. His life remained stuck, and the choices, the voices, would haunt his life forever.

The Three Strangers
Maddie Kwasnick

The sound of the bullet ricocheted off the walls, unacknowledged by the sleeping city. Just below the horizon sat the sun, casting a faint light into the darkness, chasing the night away. Everyone was either asleep or old enough to know the implications of such a sound. But she was only eight years old. Blinded by innocence and tempted by the heightened curiosity of her young age, she took small, quick steps toward the end of the block and peered around the corner. The trash-littered alley, shrouded in the morning fog, resembled the dead end of a gauntlet. An expiring yellow street light flickered overhead, illuminating the vague form of a collapsed man. Panic rose in her chest, and she let out a strangled scream as she ran toward his nearly lifeless body. She stood over him, his warm, sticky blood staining her white ballet flats as her mind spiraled out of control in horror.

"Somebody help him!" she screamed, begging for a response. No one came. Her eyes fell to the man, who was struggling to breathe as blood trickled slowly out of the side of his mouth. Silent tears spilled from his eyes while the light inside of them began to fade slowly. She looked frantically down the street, but the culprit had long since fled into the shadows of the city. This man was going to die, and there was nothing she could do to save him. The realization tore mercilessly at her heart, ripping it in two. She could only wait with him, she decided, sitting down on the cold asphalt next to him and taking his large hand in her much smaller one. So this is death, she thought, watching him as hot tears rolled down her cheeks and mixed with his on the filthy alley floor.

She was two years old when she lost her mother, too young to recall her face or the cause of her death. As her curiosity grew with age, however, she began to question her father about the whereabouts of her mother. Each time she asked, anguish would flit through his eyes for a fraction of a moment before he masked it with a convincing smile. His response was always the same. Her mother had flown to heaven, he said, but she must not worry, because she had become an angel and watches over both of them. This was how the girl knew

death. In her eyes, it had always been an unfortunate, but beautiful occurrence. Her father painted the idea with light until it practically shined. He never told her that her mother drove off a bridge, and she always wondered why he became silent when they drove across that same bridge on the way to school. One time, she insisted he divulge more details of her mother's death, but he only shook his head and repeated the scripted story he had recited for years. Her innocence was preserved, but she never really knew death until that morning.

The man's hand trembled in hers. More tears streamed down her cheeks as her previous conception of death melted inside of her. This was not beautiful, and it was clear that the man was not going to grow wings and fly away like she had imagined. She thought of his family, his friends, perhaps his spouse. They would never see him again, never hear his voice or feel his touch. She wondered if he was a good man, although she supposed that it does not matter. Good or bad, everyone meets the same end. She wondered if this is how her mother left her, suffering as the final moments of her life flashed before her eyes in a chaotic kaleidoscope of confusion and agony. Slowly, the color began to leave the world around her. A patch of green grass growing miraculously out of a crack in the street faded to a light gray, and the red bricks turned black as ashes. The monochromatic haze spilling over the city seemed to force the rising sun backward in time as it sank below the horizon. The man's breathing slowed. The light had fled from his eyes completely now, and he grasped the girl's hand tightly as the face of death approached him. After one more rasping breath, she watched as death took him in its arms and disappeared with him forever. She could only hope that he would turn into an angel.

Walking the Neighborhood
Iris Papin

Your hair is a deep, auburn whisky.
The same color as violin rosin left in a dusty cabinet, light
Illuminating the insecure insides.
Funnily enough, I've never noticed it
Until this moment,
This moment in which your hair has been
Fermenting in a stew of funeral lilies.
Has it always been that particular shade? I rewind
My brain-tape and think of a time Before
When there were no lilies to enhance everything.
We are walking through the neighborhood.
Over here, we see the little twig woman
With the angular bones protruding from her funny,
Vintage clothes. She is
Picking up the never-ending shreds of bark and
Sinew (weapons of war) from her front yard.
There's also the eleven-year-old boy who sits on his deck
Right behind the lake, quietly weaving his fingers
Into his guitar strings.
Finally, I have enough scenery-clay to work with here.
Has your hair color come to me yet?
I picture, in my mind's eye, your face
In the days Before, when we still had a
Neighborhood to walk through:
Whisky hair, still there,
Lilies- no. (eyes glow)

A Wednesday Night

Danie Leyshon

Nothing takes me, slowing the pace
Taking its time, taking its space
Spiders and cobwebs are found in their place
Searching for that which is not there
The thought and meaning they are aware
Must exist, but is found elsewhere
But eyes grow here and not over there
Here where falling in dark is your now
But might as well be the year around
And you know it's not right, but son sit tight
"Your brother's for a skeleton," they say
Who will not make it to the next day
But stay please stay until there is day
For bones without flesh are better than the rest
Of nothing and less; this is for the best

sometimes I forget I knew you
Johanna Hall

sometimes I forget I knew you
and I think that's for the best
(sometimes) (maybe) (I suppose)
other times I remember—
maybe too much.
how the room sounded like velvet and
you didn't like the rug ("too alarming")
and I was always enough (for someone else).
and then there are the in-betweens,
the one-time-this-thing-happened kinds of conversations,
those I-know-you-from-somewhere's, that board game you always beat me at
even though
I cheated.
as if the game pieces were secrets.
as if I remember the rules.

sometimes when I cried
you said the personification of the causes of my anxiety would help me cope
and I didn't say that I went to therapy too (so I know all your tricks)
and I didn't say that this room could sing
and I didn't say that my shaking hands were dancers and the game pieces
   were clouds
and I didn't say that in my anxiety workbook you have a star beside your name
(right up there with "open spaces" and "failure")

my eyes flicker like an undecided motel sign
unsure about the vacancy
(I don't know if you're staying another night)

I said "don't be a stranger"
as if I ever knew you in the first place.

you said "this isn't the answer"
as if I asked.
as if I don't already know
that you only hold what things aren't the answers.
as if I don't know process of elimination.
as if my illness doesn't fill every hole inside me
with the wrong answers
already.

how can I trust my gut when all it ever
says is abort mission.
how can I follow my heart when it's living
wherever the opposite of healing is.

I stopped ripping off my fingernails and decided to let them grow out
and yesterday I had to ask someone to open a soda can for me. like fixing
   self-destruction never opened a can.
like getting healthy doesn't mean easy.
like having ten nails instead of eight doesn't get you praise.

and I let my tears grow into ghosts
and I scattered the game pieces on that rug you hated
and I live in the in-betweens now.
and sometimes I don't even remember that
sometimes I forget I knew you.
and I think that's for the best.

The War We Wage

Bailey Logan

Inspired by Julie Mehretu's painting Diffraction,

In our minds
Swooping lines with patches of yellow peeking through become fire,
Straight lines become bullets,
Groups of dots become soldiers,
Dots of red become blood,
A vantage point becomes lights from a helicopter
   that will never reach those in need.
In our mind, a painting becomes conflict, war.

Is this all we are able to see?
The pain we have caused others
In each encounter the mistakes we make,
Instead of the laughter we inflict.

Our conscience
Never letting us forget
The war we waged on others.
Haunting us in our moments of joy and pain,
It is a silent whisper always there
To remind us to make amends.

But after those amends, are we still broken?
Unable to see the good, only the bad.
From the moment we are born, are we cynicists?
Or are we scared by this wretched world
Into believing the lies.

What if you look past the war, the fire, the pain?
What if we look to the helicopter
Coming to save those in need.
What if it reaches us?
What if we get out?
Will we ever be able to see the light?

Our Soldiers

Corin Saint Ours

We don't create heroes we destroy them

We send them off unsuspecting of the horror
they will face

We tear down heroes and build them into monsters they aren't
They have no fear, no love, no passion

They are machines that had a soul but have had it hollowed out from within

They come to peace with death as an escape

Death is something that they know cannot be controlled by themselves

Death is a tool that they wield with no remorse

Death is nothing for they know of hell on earth

A little whistle in the wind forces them to cower

A little pain forces them onward

A little hope is what drives them

But they're heroes

But they are the brave who watch over us while we lay sleeping

But no one cares

How have we abandoned them? While they cry in the darkness we applaud them

How did we drive them to the point of insanity, a point where they cannot carry on without killing

How have we been convinced to let our heroes go forth in conquest but come back with despair

Do we laugh when they speak of their sorrows because we long to suffer with them?

Do we admire them because of what they have done or what they have become?

Do we see them as our protectors or as a dog that we pet occasionally?

We take our heroes of home and make them into heroes of horror

Why?

Hope
Matthew Farina

Weather report
Tornado spreading,
Everyone's dreading,
No one can figure out how to stop it.
Everyone gather in one big pit,
Our leader said,
Our one and only leader,
But now all his leadership work
Could go down the drain if we die.
We wait in the pit.
Everyone is having trouble breathing,
Hearts beating,
Eyes white with fear,
Waiting,
Waiting,
Hoping it will pass with no harm,
What little chance that it will pass
With no harm done.
We still have hope in our eyes
And our hearts,
But in our mind we realize what little chance that it will pass,
With no harm done.
It wrenched the boards from their nails,
The nails rusty in their defeat.
It's predicted to spread across the country
And destroy everything in its path.
Our beautiful little land
That we call
America.

Here it comes,
Winds swirling,
Destroying land.
We think in our minds,
What little chance that it will miss us.
Hope
That is what brought us so far,
And it will bring us through this.
My hand flies in the air,

Dust into my eyes
As I fly.
In my country,
Across the sea from the tornado,
We call our country Iran.
I watch the only TV in our land,
Everyone watching the pretty little weather reporter
Do her job,
Talking about the tornado
That is destroying the other side of the world
Hope

Al Hudaydah

Kiran Klubock-Shukla

A light flares out
red against dusk gray
The huddled men and women start
but quickly return to their positions
A home of rubble, hewn by the
Monotonous sounds in a listening city
A city broken by foreign bombs
and national anger
The radio speaks of sickness
Of dirty water and death
Buzzing against the crackle of fire
The whine, then hollow drum sounds again
And the people stir
Settle against the vast ridges of stone
The light recedes into the darkness

South Sudan

Isaac Francis

Peace
We always pray for Peace

We always fight for Peace

But will we ever experience Peace?

Peace

Freedom from hostile aggression

Sometimes I think my cousins will never know what peace means

Am I selfish for being glad I was born in a Peaceful country?

Peace

My father always says one day there will be Peace

But what if it never happens?

Is it something we have to become accustomed to?

Peace

Fighting everyday to survive
Not knowing if you'll live to see next year

Hopeless

We always pray for Peace

We always fight for Peace

But will we ever experience Peace?

The Word

Andy Packwood

It all began with an H.

Yes, the letter H.

As in hungry. Or hippopotamus.

How odd, of all twenty-six letters, that it would be an H. What would come of such aninnocent letter? For there were more mature letters in the alphabet - A, S, T, and Z, to name afew. But... why an H?

Logan did not know. Neither did the rest of his 4th Block Algebra II class. His teacher,Mr. Kowalski, seemed even less certain. However, Logan was far from being afraid, for he hadseen much more frightening things in his dark and blurry past. Frightening things, such as:

The Blair Witch Project.

Donald Trump getting elected.

Even his very own mother, butt-naked in the bathtub.

The plastic bag of adhesive bubble letters now contained one sticker less. This harmlesscharacter, H, ascended like a zombie from the dead, gently hovered across the classroom,winding in, out, and around the students' desks. The looks on the kids' faces were yet morehorrifying images to behold. Faces of uncertainty, expressions of terrified doubt.

What exactly was going on?

"Who... who did that?" Mr. Kowalski yelled out at the class, having noticed the stickerjust inches away from his eyes as he was scribbling an algebraic formula onto the whiteboard.

The classroom was utterly and eerily silent.

He frantically waved his fists above the levitating letter as if to detect a hidden string. The search came up empty handed. "Answer me... now!" Mr. Kowalski shouted. He was not a very kind person in the first place, but this perplexing situation only made it worse. The stickersealed itself onto the board, its plastic backing peeling off and dwindling to the motionless floor.

"No... nobody did anything..." whispered a brave soul from the back of the room. Of all people, it was more than surprising to see the usually introverted Timmy speak up.

Mr. Kowalski narrowed his infuriated eyes at the poor freshman. "No one shall be exiting this classroom until we find out which one of you punks pulled this foolish prank on me!"

Nobody could've guessed what came next. From out of the same Ziploc bag, the letter E floated on over, this time diverging its path so it defied gravity right in front of Mr. Kowalski's long, witchlike nose.

E then found her place next to H.

"Who's doing this!?" Mr. Kowalski boomed. Rage seemed the only emotion he felt now.

"I demand an answer, AT ONCE!"

"Did you, like, not, like, just see it hover in, like... *midair*?" questioned the pretentious and stuck-up Karen. According to most everyone, she was a real jerk. But her words did have meaning when none of the other children's could escape their own mouths.

"I'm not an idiot, *Karen*," Mr Kowalski sneered, mocking her voice and grinding his off-white teeth at the end, "For your horrendous attitude you can join me for detention, after we figure out which one of you rascals is playing games with me..."

Karen rolled her eyes, then smacked her head on the desk in dramatic frustration. A drawn-out period of skittish shuffling and tense terror plagued the meantime, until the next incident came to be.

A new letter this time. It was an L.

The message on the board now spelled H-E-L. The students were becoming more and more anxious, fear playing with the strings on their nervous hearts as a puppeteer would do with his marionettes. The oh-so-intrepid Mr. Kowalski, too, was slightly uneasy.

Logan, as one would expect, remained steadfast.

He hadn't moved an inch, not even twitched a muscle, the entire time.

Another L came drifting out of the godforsaken bag, meandering and wandering throughout the room like an asteroid in orbit. At long last the letter

found its designated place, spelling both disaster and what appeared to be the ultimate, completed word.

H-E-L-L.

Hell.

Someone, or something, just spelled out "Hell" onto the whiteboard.

This was not good. Not good at all.

Timmy started crying. Karen wet herself. The devout Jonah whipped out his makeshift Bible and began to pray. Those that had been napping were now trapped inside a harrowing nightmare while the other students squirmed out of their seats and backed away from the front of the room. Impulsively, Mr. Kowalski dashed out the door, screaming more childishly than one would expect from an adult like him. One by one, the rest of the class followed suit, spilling into the hallway as if they were being chased by giant, man-eating spiders.

But one remained. One to see where this mess would all truly end. One to see how things might shake out. One to see the rest of the word. One undeniably, indisputably, irrefutably courageous kid.

Logan sat in his chair, pondering over this strange occurrence.

And then it happened.

The final letter, just as mysteriously, just as crazily, just as unbelievably as the first four times, emerged from the plastic bag and made its way to the whiteboard. An O.

The message was clear now. The stage was set.

The word was…

Hello.

A pale, translucent ghost materialized, a joyful smile fashioned on its adorable little face.

"Why did everyone leave?" it asked, cheerfully.

Logan grinned back.

"Hell if I know."

Radioactive Ghost of Kilkenny

James O'Brien

March on, the Radioactive Ghost of Kilkenny.
And march he does.

The man chose to sit.
His family had chosen the chair.
And as he sat he looked up
A cobweb falling from the ceiling
Landed upon his face with a soft "Hello."

And still forward he goes.
Forward goes the Radioactive Ghost of Kilkenny.

Neil took the clippings from the newspaper.
There weren't any blue pins left.
This was not good.
The red pins fell to the floor
Swiped down by a
Leprous hand.
Overweight and bulbous.

Ever onward, the Radioactive Ghost of Kilkenny

The grass dies beneath his feet.
Because of both particle expulsion
And mystic necroticism.

"Buy a pot, buy a pot," she said to Will.
"Sell your bowl to your mother.
Perhaps she'll buy it."
Ceramic found its way to Will's temple
And an ambulance found its way to Will

The Radioactive Ghost of Kilkenny, march on by.

Not More, But Why

Yndeiah Kilby

The hands on a clock go round and round seamlessly with no beginning or end.
Not stopping for the crying baby begging for food in a encrypted language
Nor the broken athlete sitting on the bench wondering "why me?"

For this thing called time is a constant I ask.
Why does it never bend to the will of man for he has no choice but to live beneath it?

People pray to its creator
The man himself that set its lethal hands In motion.
They say, Oh God please give me more.
More time with my loved ones
More time within this precious moment
More, More, More is all He hears.
But in return we hear nothing.

So I ask the very thing itself.
Dear Time,
With you I have gained strength and knowledge
With you I have gained memories and love.
For this I am thankful.

But why do you take more than you give?
Why do you grant immortality to one man?
Why do you grant more of yourself to those that do not deserve you gifts?

I ask to seek understanding for this
is my only request.
I do not ask of more, I only ask why.

My God, My God, I Forsake You
Jennifer Bui

"My God, my God, oh, why have You forsaken me," i whispered in delirium, senses swollen with morose anger. The clergy, bestowed with privileges of being your messengers and those who love you near angelic devotion, allows corruption to violently breed in their veins: innocence lost, gold for salvation, lily-white blood spilt on the soiled ground on which we blindly trample the corpses of justice.

Is this penance for the sins of old? For the fall of light? Is our enslavement to life your joy? Do You feel any pity or pain for us, Your children, whom You have loved so dearly to send Your only son to the midnight angel, to the lords of the netherworld flames, eternal in their cackling of damnation? All things are possible through You, so why is my faith not restored, only further mutilated? Your soldiers murder defenseless towns, lovers imprisoned and executed for their purity, Your supposed saints who abandon the weak for pride; who knew that holiness was so sinful?

Like Jesus on the cross, my heart is nailed to a crossroad, reluctant to betray but also to stay. Silver burns my eyes as my reflection questions me; what should i do? Remain for a thorny love from a being that can't hear my pleas nor read my entrails for an augury of my conflicted mind, or abandon my preset path of a religious person, my tie to so many other strangers? Promises from a superior figure are as worthless as a childhood promise, forgotten and lied about over time; one deception is worth a thousand needles, and my essence is already stabbed and punctured worse than Mary's seven-daggered heart.

You are my god no more, for vultures heed your word as pure and just. If god's a slave to blood and sacrifice, then he and the devil emperor should share the glacial lake. Vultures judge not of mortality nor divinity, just like you who tortures without a care. No longer will my heart be chained with permafrost or my soul weep tears of jagged garnet. Do not forgive me for my betrayal; this Judas has no regrets.

    I choose treason, a life with no subservience that demands a price from the living, a life in which I'm not suffocated with the last warm sighs of lovers as they drown in a sea of double suicides, desperate hands clawing at my ankles with black rose nails as failing lungs are submerged in a deluge of boiling sea foam. Punish me with your stones and fiery stakes, I care not the method.

    I'll live my life of heresy and I'll live for me. My god, my god, I forsake you.

Unknown

Lily Van Liew

Religion has always been something...unknown
Celebrating Christmas and Easter, never for religious reasons
More for Santa Claus and the Easter Bunny
Growing up without religion
I've have such a 'blank canvas'
To explore many different forms of God

So many different religions around the world
Seeing so many people worshiping something they believe in
I realized a long time ago,
I don't have to believe in one certain idea of what God is

There is something bigger than us,
Could be God, but who knows?
Could be Greek Gods, Muslim God, Allah, or Hindu Gods, Krishna,
    Vishnu, or Ganesha
God can be whatever a person believes him (or her) to be

No need to hate one another just for different beliefs
The God we worship is fine
No punishment for beliefs or lack thereof,
Just appreciate one another's religion
Whatever higher power there is would want us to love one another
And live in harmony.

Religion is something no one person can really explain
But it is something we all need in our lives
Every person on earth needs love, compassion, heartfelt emotion
And to believe in something...
Even if it is not a God

anxiety and religion in eleven parts
McKenzie Hall

number one
i have spent nights coating prayers in tears and flinging them
at my ceiling and wondering how much helium
i need to cry to make them float up to God and if i take one step
He will take the other ninety nine but i cannot move my feet

number two
i run each sprint faster than the last even after my lungs collapse
because there is always someone watching and i cannot read
their minds but mine is telling me they think less of me
if i am not the fastest or the smartest or the prettiest or perfect

number three
theoretically seventeen years of reinforcement should solidify
a belief system but my very pores are doubting and atoms are mostly
air so when i touch this table for stability i am trusting my body to more
air and nothing really feels real anymore

number four
if i ignore you in the halls it is not because i hate you it is because
my lips are sewed shut by indecision and the worst that could happen
is you don't say hi back and even then it is probably just because
you didn't hear me but probably is not a comforting word

number five
my lips say i am a christian and my heart is screaming to be a christian
and my fingers hold my bible like a liferaft and it tells me
mustard seed faith is good enough but is that overridden by shame
the size of a small planet because i am told shame is a sin

number six
i do not know how to explain to you why certain noises make me feel
static and i know you will love me anyways but i still cannot
reconcile imperfection and love and your lips are saying all the right
   things
but my mind is still managing to fill my veins with fear

number seven
in the bible God says do not fear 365 times at least that is what i saw on
pinterest and if that is not enough to calm my turbulence what is enough
i am defined by afraid and i have been adopted by Him but my mind is
lingering on who gave me up was i not good enough

number eight
i am writing an elegy for myself even though i am not dead yet it goes
i'm sure she was good at something and somebody must have loved her
but we don't need to name names and you can tell me i am wrong but
to be completely honest i probably will not believe you

number nine
anxiety is not poetic it is a religion i do not know how to not
believe depression is not imaginary it is dogma and i have been
brainwashed say the right words and i will be broken say nothing
in the right tone of voice and i will be at your feet bleeding

number 10

i have spent nights wishing to be icarus maybe free falling was worth the
warmth and maybe at the end he found answers and maybe
he is remembered for his idiocy but at least he is remembered and i wonder
did he find God in the face of the sun is that why he flew

number 11

maybe there is peace in the clouds.
i'll keep looking.

This is Hell

Cesca Grazioli

   I. Birth
I wake from an elusive sleep,
gasping for breath and finding only fire.
I am born of embers,
of charcoal hearts,
of bare, burnt legs.
I cry
and my mother catches the tears
until an ocean roars in her hands.
I stand on the edge,
teetering on her thumb,
numb from spray like ice,
like fire. I burn, and I plunge
deep below the surface, where
creatures of the shadows
Lurk.

   II. Fury
I observe the houses,
every one like mine,
the same dull green and gray,
weeds sprouting from the same walkways.
Identical children surround me,
every one like me,
hiding in the same closets,
playing with the same knives.
We hold twilight in our hands;
fingers bruised purple
from tapping at the windows,

hoping someone will hear.
We move as one,
ropes burning around our necks,
nooses like necklaces,
praying God,
oh God, grant us this
if nothing else.

   III. Intoxication
I move through
heat from a hundred bodies,
thick as molasses.
Feverish electricity sparkles
like fireworks,
reflected in glassy eyes
and glossy lips.
Girls in sequined skirts
pluck light bulbs
and chew them, spitting
blood into wine glasses.
Teeth nip my shoulder,
threadbare lips cracking
and spilling drunken secrets.
My body is smoke,
and liquor;
fingernails graze my back,
take hold of my wrist.
I feel the dirty needle,
sharp pinch,
then numbness,
golden heart and blackened veins.

IV. Awakening
This is hell.
I laugh and
wave my pen,
a warrior with her sword,
tearing through my skin
like paper.
I bathe
in a river of ink:
unwritten words,
and undone deeds.
I know all
and nothing will change.
This is hell.

The Evil Lake
Lily Deleo

Dragged along to another camping trip
My sister and I so wanted to skip
While our parents prepped the camping spot
Shonelle and I wandered the woods till coming across
A lake, so ugly we were shocked
A lagoon in bloom with hues of snotty green, sticky black and moldy blue
It burst with purple pus and prickled with pink loam
It curdled with chunky white and leaked with scratchy yellow foam
The stew brewed up a foul stench
Of eggs, ogre body odor, fungused feets, fumey farts and sewer dregs
We clenched our nuked noses and forced our fists inside our mouths
But the sick smell of that water lives forever inside my nostrils now
My sister heaved her tuna sandwich from her stomach to the ground
And my offended orifices sent dangerous drool, murderous mucus and toxic
    tears trickling down
Then I spotted it; a skinny, shaggy beast sporting a coat of red, orange and brown
Adorned with bulging, beady eyes roofed by a humongous brow
The small monster was spying, perched upon a far off rock
And it hopped to a closer stone the second our eyes locked
Its sneaky smile swirled and curled into a naughty knot
Sizing up what it must have thought it caught
I gave the gremlin no chance, grabbed my spewing sis and spun around
    about to bolt
But what I heard beckoned behind my back caused me to jolt
I turned to watch the word finish slipping off its slim lips
My name plopped in the pool and sunk into the abysmal abyss
My scared statue stares were answered by my still ill lil' sis
Who pointed to my beaded bracelet labeled 'Marcus'
Then Shonelle uttered, "dinguths," (cuz of her lisp)

The freaky creature chuckled in shrill and squeaky shrieks
But the pitch was cut with a deep tone that reeked distinctly of a he
The squat sir said, "Hello, how do you two do?"
"Well, alright I guess," I answered. "Until we found this gross lagoon."
"Oh, but no, the lake is lovely don't you see? The water is wondrously warm–"
"Probably cooking up bacteria in fresh, piping hot pee."
His tail spiked with agitation, "That is not how we go about our irrigation!
In fact, the precipitation comes in many colors here, and that is why the
    pool's not clear.
Each shade tastes of a different delectable flavor, so why not calm your
    unwelcome wrath and
have both a feast and a bath?"
I laughed, "Then why'd I react like I'd just had a taste of rotted ass?"
His face furled into fiery frustration fast and he blast,
"Your senses suffer strange behavior since you've never smelt nor savored
    such supernatural
scents that your bitty brain can't hope to comprehend, so it overloads,
    thinks it a threat; poor
thing's probably quite spent!"
"My mind's just fine, and it knows nasty when it sees it.
Mystical awe, nah, that ain't the reason we're wheezin' and squeezin' our noses."
"Yeah, I think mine started bleedin'." Shonelle showed her nose to the fussy,
    furry demon.
His big brow burrowed, burying his bitter eyes beneath, then open again
    they flied, revived of
courtesy and acting kind
"My sweet, the smell does not dwell once you take a dip.
The aromas all alter when you get used to it, then all you'll want to do is sip!
So come on kids, why don't we three go for a swim?"
"Unh-uh, no way, have to reject that invitation.
I bet we'd get dragged under by some vile creation.
There's gotta be about a billion malicious monstrosities, who'll find Shonelle
    and me delicious

dishes.
So I sure as hell won't go along with your wishes!"
The miffed mister bit his little lip till it formed a blister
"Silly boy," he spat, grating his tiny teeth this way and that,
"There isn't a single someone submerged who seeks to eat your meat, only someones tame and
sweet.
The lake itself is a themself- and they are really neat!"
"I don't dive into thinking things, 'specially if it thinks of me as game."
Shonelle backed me up with a simple "same," sufficiently driving home my claims
The dude did an angry jig, he tapped his puny feet, and shook his pointy hips
The wig wrapped twigs that were his limbs jittered and slithered as he threw his fit
"That's IT!" he spit.
"I'm done, I quit, now shove off you brats, you win."
And so, right then, we promptly did
As we ditched I heard the turd complain,
"I try my best, but kids these days, oh, they sure got their brains! I'm sorry lake."
The lake slopped up a sluggish sigh
And the mini mammalian replied,
"We'll have to try another time."

Stars and Streetlights/ Man on the Moon

Rafe Forward

He watched the small lights flickering below through the clouds
Shadows lived and died through roofs of trees from his perspective
He was the first man to live on the moon
Born from the stars and raised among craters and mounds
He lived alone, visiting the land below, and then shrinking back to the sky
He spent his time wading in pools of ink
Every step further in made him forget about the hour
When the sun almost disappears from the horizon and
He is thrust into view
When the sun comes out, the ink evaporates exposing him to the elements
Wind lashes his skin and light pierces his eyes
Frost seeps deep, locking his motions until sunrise
Biding his time until he can step back into the ocean
The one that he pulls back and forth
The one whose bubbles swarm around him and carry him home
And whose waves push him back to shore reintroducing him to the world
Not born from foam and warm light, but from the whirlpools and thunder
His dreams are vivid
Visions of running
Leaving his world behind for an endless array of stars and streetlights
But the lights that flicker through the clouds create shadows
And like the shadows, his dreams fade and he has to return
Back to the craters and mounds

The Moon's Beckoning
David Colavincenzo

The Moon's light shone through the open glass roof of the Grand Cathedral of Coricea, falling onto the statue at the end of the Chapel. The statue depicted Kilawa, Daughter of the Moon, the first Black Alpha Dragon. Green flames lined her chest and a green ember glowed from the top of her forehead. Her body was smooth and deceptively soft. The scales resembled cloth and her wings were spread out, allowing the Cathedral's attendants to bask in the might of the first Daughter of the Moon. The High Priestess kneeled before the statue and began to pray as the bell tower of the city outside began to toll. The candles were lit on the altar, as well as on the pathway to the statue itself. As the High Priestess began to pray, the doors of the Cathedral swung open, and Lawrence the Scholar appeared and ran down the aisle. His face was as pale as fresh snow. He was dressed in his robes, one sleeve was torn, exposing a bleeding arm. Startled by his appearance, the High Priestess stood and raised her hand,

"Lawrence, what is going on?"

Lawrence's face was expressionless until he cracked a small smile that exposed his pristine teeth.

"Has the Moon ever beckoned to you before, High Priestess?"

"No. The Moon's Beckoning is a sacred event that happens when it sees a possible host for yet another of its offspring. Another Calamity Dragon to be specific. As a scholar, you know it happened to the first king of Magnis Paradine, who brought Kilawa to us. Why? Do you think the Moon has beckoned to you?"

A strong breeze filled the worship space, extinguishing the candles. Then the light of the Moon became shrouded by clouds and the flames on the statue began to fade. The High Priestess turned her head towards the statue in awe. Turning back to Lawrence, who had moved closer to the altar, she spoke.

"Lawrence, speak! What has happened?"

"The Moon has called upon me to oversee the creation of the next Calamity Dragon. I know what is going on underneath this Cathedral. I know of the beast you are creating. It is to be released into the city."

"Even if you are claiming to be the overseer of the next Calamity Dragon, I will not in my right mind allow you to release it."

"Then you are not denying the existence of another dragon beneath the Cathedral."

"There is no point in denying the truth, but I will not allow you to see the dragon and then release it onto the populus. Do you not remember the destruction Kilawa caused when she was brought forth into the world? It took years, decades for Magnis Paradine to rebuild. It took even longer for the Church to regain the trust of the people, and I will not allow you to squander the trust of the citizens and the funds they provide because you believe you are the next host. We will not release Phoroneus."

Lawrence moved closer to the High Priestess.

"It already has a name! It must be close to hatching from its shell!" Lawrence yelled, rushing for the High Priestess and grabbing her by the collar of her cape. "How do I get down to the dragon!"

The High Priestess let out a chilling scream as Lawrence dragged her across the tile floor of the Grand Cathedral.

"If you kill me, you will never find it!" she screamed, hoping to deter Lawrence.

"Very well. I will not kill you, but you will show me the dragon."

"Do I have your word that you will not release it onto the public?" she asked.

"You have my word," Lawrence replied, releasing the High Priestess.

Standing, the High Priestess led Lawrence to a secret lift that was hidden behind the statue of Kilawa. The clouds had now cleared, and the Moon's light shone on the statue. Once again the flames of Kilawa ignited once more. The lift descended to the depths of the cathedral until it reached a large cavern. Lawrence looked out the frame of the open-sided lift and laid his eyes upon the next Calamity Dragon.

"Phoroneus is the first White Omega Dragon ever recorded in the history of Magnis Paradine," the High Priestess said.

The dragon's size was larger than Kilawa ever was. Its wings emerged from slightly behind the front shoulders. They were massive. They resembled wings of birds, the tips being separated from the wing itself. They were a light blue, a crystal blue. Unlike Kilawa, Phoroneus stood on all fours. In front of its shoulders, crystallized armor covered the joints. Its claws were large guillotines. Smaller wings protruded from its legs, just above the ankles. A long neck supported Phoroneus's head, considerably smaller than the rest of the body. This neck bore crystal blades that emphasized the dragon's glorious head. Its snout was rounded at the end, and two sky blue eyes lined each side. On top of its head was a white and blue crown-like mantle made of crystals that extended out on all sides.

Once the lift reached ground level, The High Priestess grabbed one of the guards' spears and drove it into Lawrence's back, shattering his spine.

"I know Jupiter beckoned you to kill Phoroneus." She paused. "The Second Grand Cleansing has come. Those who have stopped looking towards the Moon and the Stars have sinned," the High Priestess said. Then, there was a flash of white light in the cave and Phoroneus was gone.

The High Priestess and her deacons watched from the safety of the Grand Cathedral as Phoroneus ravaged Magnis Paradine. Citizens scrambled towards the front gate to escape the blaze, only to find the gate locked and guards armed to prevent entry.

"What changed your mind about releasing Phoroneus?" one deacon asked.

"Because Phoroneus beckoned to me. Phoroneus is the embodiment of the Moon."

Aphrodite in Birth & Death
Astrid Weisend

The sea foam stung her with small shards of sand to chorus with the salt in her eyes that she didn't yet know to keep closed. She was born confused, the ocean stained communion wine from a father's death, wondering why she arrived on earth with weeping maturity, untouched by innocence. Her first breaths were drowning, her first thoughts death. Thus, Aphrodite came alive.

Within the instant, washed up, coughing on shore, the gods loved her. Somehow, despite exemplifying deific emotion, all love and rage, they never registered her as being the same as them, though she always tried to connect. Within the day, she was married. She didn't even know his name, just picked him out of a lineup of cherubic faces with strong noses, a whispered hint and subtle jab by a woman used to being queen. Hephaestus appeared the least cherubic and strong, and he never proved that initial assessment wrong. Eventually, though, everyone looked the same to her, all broken apart in adoration.

Desperate to find something people would struggle to love about her, she walked the thin line of ichor on a father's throat as his son harvested the throne, waiting for the gap to widen, new rivets to appear. If she followed the paths far enough, she knew she could find where all broke apart, find where she began. But that only worked in memories that were not her own, only ever able to experience undying devotion, as those she played with gave way as soon as her feet landed.

Then, it began. Slowly, when she went outside the mountains, she noticed her own appearance replicated with every new goddess, nymph, and niaid, as every deity remembered at once that they could change their forms to find beauty, slipping her face on like a brightly dyed cloth, like hiding from monsters under a mother's skirt.

Faster, her own features changed, ever so slightly, to somehow reach a new form of perfection. Living felt like pins and needles, constantly evolving while the other gods shifted in line behind her, following in her footrace back towards the ocean, always getting purer in shape than her birth. The curse of being a god is always having to be the epitome of what you rule, and she wondered when she would reach the pinnacle of creation; what would make her jump off.

The outside world became a horrific maze of mirrors with jagged edges designed to cut only her. She didn't want the pain for herself, and her husband, Hephaestus, told her she physically hurt to look at. Something about love demands contradiction, the dissection of instinct, and the brain can only process so much. He was the only one she could talk to anymore, wounded as he was to be ugly forever. Birth scarred them both, people unknowingly ridiculing their hurt with their mundane description of how the pain persisted.

Hiding only works for so long, even less so when you are a goddess beloved by the people, and the world called her out. Within moments of her illuminating the cloudy, gold pillars of the mountain, as the crowd watched in loving fixation, she was gone. Not all the way, no, but rapidly disappearing as each particle of her being was stolen onto the faces filled with tears at how blinding she was, for the only thing more beautiful than perfection was knowing that it was lost; the impression left behind.

Eventually, all that remained was her wide, terrified eyes as she took in the confusion scattered across the earth. The pupils kept on getting greater, wider, brighter until Hephaestus turned away, fearing she would swallow them up, frying his retinas with universal sorrow as the amplifier. Surely, this was the light of death calling everyone to it; she was inescapable. The rest watched without blinking, vision closing in on something awful, but not willing to look away, as the tragedy of her vanishing was somehow better than her life. Then, the last of her dispersed into the youngest dryads desperate for notice, swirling into everyone's thoughts like blood diffused in water, as gods cannot die but must suffer their due for eternity. The water might run clear again, but there would be iron in the brine.

So, everyone watched in mirrors and dreamed, waiting for their bones to become ethereal in slivers of night, become the peak of being or drowning with hope of emerging fresh and complete. As much as they tried to pull the tides closer, using the sorrow that had once glimmered like ichor in the sea, their faces could never twist like Aphrodite meeting death again, seeing son and father cut and bleed.

ecstatic fragmentation

Bryn Malone

light spills out of cracks and you laugh
smile
dance through the ruins of a dying world
we are gods
holy and wholly untouchable
dust and smoke turn light tangible
it winks from shards of glass and spills from your fingertips
and you turn to me
sharp burning light too bright in your eyes
and say it's over
and say we've won
and I think to myself
as you flicker through ruined grandeur
and grin in the face of your power
destruction is not triumph
pyrric victories don't count
rome wasn't built in a day but it burned in one
the spartans said e tan e epi tas
with your shield or on it
come back victorious or dead
and now I know
we are neither the victorious nor the dead
there are no bargains between lions and men
and the dying world roars
our mothers held us too tight
the river styx will not wash us away
and yet in our strength is our downfall
if a tree falls in a forest does it even make a sound?
if a god dies unseen were they ever really there?

Willow's Deal

Henry Kipps

Willow stumbled through the Deepwoods, the moon full and heavy overhead, casting its darkness through the trees. The forest curled in around her, its natural defenses reaching out to slow her progress; she already bled from several scrapes by the thorns, but she pressed on, belligerent.

Hours of effortful trudging saw her at a clearing—it was out of place, the trees on its border packed tightly as castle bricks. The stars shone here, in contrast to the absolute black from which she'd come. Willow traversed the intricate pattern of flowers on the ground, foot after foot, till she reached the center of the clearing; there, a tree stump protruded from the center of a small pool of water. Fireflies hung in the air, lights dancing, tainting the cool air bluish gray.

Willow reached for a pouch at her belt, pulling out a handful of rose petals. She scattered them over the pool, and a wind blew in from behind her, whipping her hair past her shoulders and picking up the petals. They swirled up to the sky, and she turned her head to watch them disappear into the distance. When she turned back, she was no longer alone.

"One such as you must have come an awful long way to seek me, young one." A lady was sitting on the once vacant stump, her bare feet just barely touching the water below, sending out small ripples. She wore a green-trimmed white dress, its flowing sleeves draped over long arms that ended in feral, curved claws. Wind that Willow couldn't feel carried a head of long, curling hair off to the side, and her face, green and freckled, smiled, selfishly.

"One such as me has an awful lot to gain, and precious little to lose," Willow replied, looking straight into the lady's discolored eyes.

"One such as you always has something to lose," said the lady. "Whether you know it or not."

Willow straightened. "I didn't come for wordplay."

"Fair enough, little one. Let us move along. What is your name, and what do you seek?"

"I am Willow Tenebrae, and I seek power."

"Power?" The lady drummed her claws against her cheek. "You certainly are an interesting one, Willow Tenebrae. The corrupt of heart comprise the Seekers of Power, nine out of ten; yet, your heart harkens towards justice, not conquest."

Willow set her jaw. "The High Lord's men took my village. My family."

The lady's smile curved up at the ends, sweet and masking. "And you would avenge their lives—their work?"

Willow shook her head. "The dead are dead; I seek to save those that still live. Alburkakaj and his men shall harm no more."

"This power you wish for... I can grant you it, for a price. Are you willing to engage in Covenant?"

"Yes. As I said, I have nothing to lose."

The smile turned to a laugh, and, in an instant, the clearing erupted into a bright green light. Vines crawled from the ground, arching over the two of them, wrapping up towards the moon, spelling out runes against the trees. The lady raised off the tree stump, raised into the air, splaying her jade arms to the side. Her hair grew twice its length, mimicking the shape of her billowing skirt. Rose thorns flowed from her open throat and sewed her lips shut, but her voice still rang out true, echoing off the trees.

"Know, Seeker Willow Tenebrae of Power, that you speak to Melisande Mirai, Archfey Queen of the Deepwoods. Know, Savior Willow Tenebrae of the Living, that until you find your desire fulfilled, or until you find your life forfeit, all that you speak is henceforth contract: unretractable, unescapable, unsilenced. Thus the Queen presents the Covenant, as her part. Does the Seeker accept the terms, as hers?"

Willow swallowed, watching in apprehension as the vines squirmed like tentacles above her head. "I accept the terms."

The world shook; Willow screamed; the moon spasmed in the green sky; Melisande laughed through her stitched lips; ancient, powerful scriptures wrote themselves up and down the vines, the trees, Willow's skin; everything snapped to black.

Willow stood before the High Lord, illuminated by the golden candelabra and chandeliers throughout the throne room. Her bare feet clung to the red carpet beneath her, and her eyes glowed with the soft pink light of the fey-touched. Alburkakaj, sat on the throne in front of her, took a moment of silence for the guards that lay dead on either side of him. Closing his eyes, taking a deep breath, he spoke.

"To think; the two most powerful humans on the continent, both doomed to die on the same day. Sheila above truly has a sense of poetry to her workings."

Willow frowned. "You think with an awfully narrow mind. There is so much power in the world if you know where to look."

"You would disagree, then?" Alburkakaj laughed, deep and throaty. "The High Lord of the only empire in history to conquer this half of the globe, and the fey-touched girl who mastered her gifts like no other before her? Who else comes close?"

"Had you asked yourself that question sooner, maybe you would have stopped me. Your selfishness brought death to your doorstep."

"Selfishness?" Alburkakaj gestured outwards, motioning beyond the throne room's walls. "I brought innovation, technology, and prosperity to all the people of this continent!"

"You brought nothing but death and cruelty!" Willow spat, her eyes flaring up. "How many did you kill? When did you lose count?"

Alburkakaj looked down at one of the guards, who had a hole in his chest the size of a tree trunk. "When did you?"

"I kill for justice; you only kill for yourself!"

"And where, exactly, are you drawing that line?" Alburbakaj reached into his blood-spattered robes and pulled out a small dagger, sharp and curved and made of gold. "When you look in the mirror, I'm sure you see a noble fighter for what is good and just. But I look before me, and I see a little girl throwing the biggest temper tantrum that Sheila's sweet Earth has ever seen." He paused for a moment, turning the knife over in his hand, rubbing his thumb over the flat of the blade. "I see a girl who whined and whined until someone gave her what she wanted, without thinking of the consequence. I see a girl who threw her life away just to end so many more. I see a girl who, truly, is thinking with such a narrow, narrow mind."

Willow was fuming. "You're wrong."

"Am I?" Alburkakaj raised his dagger, and plunged it into his heart, slumping in the throne.

Willow let out a roar, magic exploding around her in bursts of anger.

"Well, he certainly knows how to make an exit."

Willow whipped around, training her eyes on Melisande. She was floating slightly above the ground, flowers and vines curling up through the castle's flooring.

"Tell me, Willow Tenebrae; are you satisfied?"

"No," she said.

"I'd imagined as much. High Lord Alburkakaj… for all that he was wrong, he was right about you." Melisande snapped her fingers, and Willow died.

Rattlesnake Reveries
Abigail Connelly

The dead do their midnight dance,
Shaking and swaying and swirling,
Like fiery flames in an open room,
Their bodies empty but their glasses full.
If you listen, you can hear them sing,
They sing of petals on flowers and birds in the sky,
Don't forget where you came from.
They give thanks to the earth,
To the dirt from which we rose and to which we will return.
How do you walk past a graveyard without breathing?
Open your lungs and feel the shaking ground,
Listen to the music of the mortals,
The claps and stomps of past and present,
They dance for you.
Do you feel their hands clawing at you from the belly of the grass?
They are reaching to greet you.
Sing songs to the shadows;
Sweet serenades for the buried.
It gets quite lonely beneath the trodden path.

concertos
Aimee Straka

i trill a shattered refrain
of satisfaction,
but some fervors never die,
only fading
into jarring harmonies
of covert loathing, half-forgotten
and yes i am mending,
so i can strum
a lullaby, a dirge of joy
on the harp of my denial,
and they will believe
that i am cured
of my ache for hunger —
am i? —
they never stop to ponder
that maybe
my chorus of self poison
      doesn't have an antidote.

agony, indecisive,
trickles through my lips,
tastes tiptoeing
on my tongue
conjure haunting melodies
of cloying sweetness,
nauseating grease,
and contempt;
or perhaps the flavors
croon concertos of beauty,

i can never seem to tell;
for my psyche is haunted
by notes twisting furiously
across the ivory keys
of my sanity, reminiscent
of cold moonlight:
dazzling in its tainted elegance,
      ferocious in its despair.

sometimes i caress my ribs,
remembering when i
could play them
with a flourish,
like a sick kind of xylophone;
some nights i wish
i still could —
i know i shouldn't —
but hunger still sits carved
into my consciousness,
lyrical tattoos
seared into my skin
and when my flesh
withered away i screamed,
frantic tears melting
from my sunken eyes,
yet i could never seem
to make myself stop.
      i wonder why sometimes
      i still can't.

Days in the Circus

Aoife Arras

White and red lights sweep the stage clean and a bass makes the tent walls shiver. The cotton curtains camouflage themselves in the moonlight. Clowns step from the shadows, red paint curling into a smile on their shiny white faces.

My feet rumble down the carpeted stairs and I peek through a square window to speculate the weather. A hallway beckons me to the kitchen. "Good morning," I say cheerfully to my father.

"Good morning," he replies. We eat breakfast together. I can feel an audience watching.

He drives me to school in our decade-old Honda Civic. I stare out the window blankly, my eyes shifting out of focus into a cloudy dimension. Music pours into the cup of my right eardrum, the left bearing silence in case my dad says something to me. He hates it when he has to repeat things. Strange, considering we both repeat the same show every day.

I walk into school with a high chin, ignoring the fact that I am five minutes late to class every day. The teachers have halted the barricade of tardies and accepted my lateness.

Class makes the batteries of the clocks die.

I stare into a tan desk, freckled with grey and white specks, and I see sand in the Saharan Desert. I see my feet sunken into hot sand.

I look out the window and see the clouds racing each other across the sky. A small pilot plane suddenly zips through the blue open. The white fluffy beings cry from their loss in the race. I stand up from my hard seat, my legs sore, and I see myself in the seat of the air vehicle.

"What are you doing?" My teacher inspects, annoyed. If only she could see what I see.

"I don't know what I'm doing. I have no idea what I'm doing." The class breaks into layers of chuckles and mumbled comments. They're laughing because everything I do is funny. I smile, because this was most definitely the reaction I was looking for. I was most definitely looking for a reaction. The sound of laughter curls into a ball in my ears, burrowing a nest that will be there all winter. The bell rings.

I eat lunch with different people every week, because I'm welcome to sit wherever. Everyone accepts free tickets to the circus. No one likes school though.

I like school. I hate the circus.

The themes of lunch conversation are similar but at different volume levels. It's brightening how their faces move when they speak, each face different, even twins. I soak in all of the novels told in the nosy cafeteria and the hectic library. These books are the ones that I read in my mind before falling asleep.

Lunch sprints away into the hands of my "friends" before I can even touch it. It's the hunger that reminds me of the time and the place and speaks to me as individual rumbles in the silence.

The time spent after school is in quiet reflection and busy work from all of my classes. My friends/peers sit with me at a round cafeteria table, as we wait to attend the dreaded swim practice. I do not dread swimming at all.

"Ugh, I really don't want to go to practice," my lips conjure. Others at the table nod in agreement. I wonder if they actually agree with me. I don't agree with myself.

We all "dread" having to go to swim practice on the way there.

Under the cool surface, there are words that I would never say. People's secrets are written along the bottom of the pool. I think about things as my arms and legs move.

When I swim long enough, I enter a realm of bliss. I can't hear anything under the water. No one is watching me.

My muscles tingle as blood rushes through them - a warm, painful feeling that I enjoy during the most difficult sets in practice. I suddenly have no need to breathe, to talk, or to think. I only swim. It makes me invincible.

My peers and my audience think of me as talkative. They don't know that inside, my real thoughts bubble and mingle, as they prefer to stay inside where it is warm.

There are many moments of the daily itinerary that I enjoy. Riding in the car is not one of them - especially when my dad is antisocial.

My eyes wander so far sometimes that they gawk at things that aren't there. I would love to talk of how I see rainbows in the white clouds or ladies in red overalls marching for more credit in this world.

Instead I see broken windows dripping in blood, bumper cars programmed to go too fast, and pale white hands reaching for the knobs to moving cars' doors.

At home I eat sometimes, and then I tread through dense atmosphere into my room, where I stare at the ceiling for hours, blankly. It has the texture of skin, slight bumps and marks here and there, but smooth overall. I'm too short to touch it, even when I stand on my bed. The side walls aren't the same. I then pace around my room, over and over, because everything is a lost act. In the dark depths of the night, my toes dance across the rugged floor.

I touch my own face as I stare into a moonlit mirror streaked with salt. I gaze at my fingers. They are smothered in white paint and red lipstick.

Living in a Broken World

Ashley Taylor

Living in this world isn't easy,
Our world is broken.

Parents get divorced,
But that's a norm for this generation.
Marriage isn't regarded as valuable,
Or even a commitment in some cases.
Our world is broken.

Wouldn't say it's my fault,
But I don't know much about commitment.
I don't like to spend too much time on just one person.
Everyone tends to be just a distraction from what's real,
And that's why,
Our world is broken.

I'm eighteen and already exhausted.
Rather be locked in my own universe,
Than waste time explaining who I am,
To a group of friends who don't understand,
Because,
Our world is broken.

Life shouldn't be wasted,
But people like to please others.
I don't have energy for that,
I just wanna be free,
No questions asked, but
Our world is broken.

Don't you see?
Staying hidden is better.
Everyone is so scared of emotion.
You express it, you're dramatic,
And if you don't, you need "help."
I just want to be me, but
Our world is broken.

Every day race is a constant conflict,
Everyone wondering if they are good enough,
Fighting for someone to care,
But failing to realize,
In technical terms, we're all the same.
Why can't we seem to see it?
It's simple,
Our world is broken.

It's quite preposterous.
We're all equally superb in our own way,
All struggling in some way,
But we like to segregate ourselves in groups,
Of equally scared, miserable, or tinted people.
How can we all want to be accepted,
But we judge when we know nothing?
How do we want to live freely,
But bash those who live differently?
How do we say, "we should all be treated the same,"
But can't come together as a whole?
Man, our world is broken.

Rusting
Brehanu Bugg

it is said that time heals all wounds
    but it makes mine deeper
i live in this ageing body
whose clockwork is starting to rust
the gears
screaming
and the hands
forgetting where they are supposed to go
until i am broken
tossed out in the streets
waiting for someone to oil up these ancient scars
and make me theirs again
but there is no oil
    just rain
the ticks
        keep
            coming
the tocks
        keep
            going
the rhythm beating along with this heart
that is about to burst
    yet the clock keeps on ticking
        and the wounds keep getting deeper

Sea-Song
Kathryn Steenburgh

An old man sits on the rocks just above a bay.

It is November in Maine. The cold is bone-chilling.

The old man does not notice. He is oblivious to it all; oblivious to the crashing waves, the eerily-whistling wind, the swiftly-turning lighthouse not far in the distance.

There is one thing, though, that the old man is not oblivious to. There is a song in the distance, carried on the wind. Old and wistful and beautiful. Old and wistful and right.

The singer's voice is light and deep at the same time; muted with distance, but cacophonous with its impact. It sinks into him, anchors a line into his chest.

Something on the other end heaves.

He draws a ragged breath, then slides haltingly down the rock's side, not caring as the sharp edges tear into his clothing and leave small scrapes on his wizened legs. He doesn't notice the scrapes sting as the saltwater hits them, or the numbness that soon sets in. He doesn't notice as the sea and the sky become more and more frenzied, the line between them becoming blurred where foaming surf hits rain-soaked air.

The man swims.

His face bobs in the water—over, under, over, under. He heaves a breath whenever he can, inhaling nearly as much water as he does air. If he could feel his limbs, they would be burning. His heart pumps harder than it has in years.

And all of a sudden, the man can no longer hear.

His body fights the wave, but unwillingly, he is pushed under. The wind is gone from his ears, the air from his throat. But the loss he feels most keenly is that of the music.

The string is gone from his chest, the fog from his brain. His body burns, finally feeling the delayed effects of his midnight swim.

This is madness, the man realizes.

He forces his now-leaden limbs into motion, arms and legs flailing awkwardly until his mouth breaches the surface. He attempts to suck in a breath just as a wave comes over him, filling his screaming lungs with pitch-black water.

With what feels like the last of his energy, the man makes one more thrust for the top. His head emerges from the surf, and he splutters and heaves. Air rushes into his lungs, and the feeling is so welcome he nearly faints.

But the victory is momentary. As soon as the water begins to trickle from his ears, a familiar tug roots itself in his chest. He feels himself slipping and tries to resist, but it's no use.

He feels his limbs begin to move half-without consent, and knows he's fighting a losing battle. He fights it for a moment; pulls his head above water and tries to find the moon. One last look, he thinks, bittersweet, but he can't see it past the thick layer of storm clouds.

Two raindrops hit his eyes in tandem, and his last glimpse of the sky is obscured. He stops resisting, and his body crashes into the waves once again.

The music overtakes him again, but this time he is even less aware. Every part of his consciousness that isn't anchored to the tune drifts. It's like a dream and a nightmare all at once; one moment it's terrifying, existential blackness, the next, a euphoric light. Underneath, far, far underneath, he can hear the pulsing beat of his heart.

As he moves, the singing begins to consume him. Somewhere inside, he knows he must be getting closer. He can feel it in his bones now, permeating his body from the inside out. It's warmth and it's cold, stillness and vibration. It's a dynamic contradiction. He's never felt so complete. He's never felt so fragmented.

Then, all at once, his vision is consumed, too. He sees something ahead; something... real. Is it real? A rock, and, on it, a woman. A woman, yet... not quite. She looks like one, but there's something odd about her. He can't register her face, not really. He's not sure if she's even really there. It's almost as if her being is shifting, features changing in rapid succession. She flickers, like her presence is divided. Like she exists in both his plane and another.

Her energy is ethereal and powerful; visible, even. She radiates light and darkness. If it's possible, he swims faster. He hadn't known it before, but he knows it now: she is his goal.

He reaches the stone where she sits. His fingers scrabble against the barnacle-crusted surface. The delicate skin, especially so waterlogged, should break, but it doesn't. Instead, his fingertips find the tiny, nearly indiscernible crevasses in the rock and he pulls himself up.

Now that he's here, so close to her, he feels nothing but giddy, manic euphoria. His eyes take in her changing form. She's turned away from him, her back facing him. He is stuck in his place.

And then she turns.

And she changes.

Suddenly, she is terrible, and he is horrified. Still, he cannot move.

And then she changes back to beautiful. Then terrible. Then beautiful, Then… then, she stops, speaks.

"You know what you must do."

As he hears the sound of her voice, an atmosphere of calm surrounds him. He does. He knows what he must do.

No longer frozen, he walks toward her. As he nears, she changes. Her indiscernible features open up and disappear, and all that is left is a warm, blinding light. He gets closer, and now he is the one who is changing. He sees his hands; the wrinkles are disappearing, skin shrinking and firming. He feels rejuvenated; better than he has in years. Instinctively, he knows he must look as he did when he was a young man. Then, he begins to shrink, and the process is going faster, faster. He twists and changes, body gone, boundaries gone…

And suddenly, he is nothing. And suddenly, he is everything.

I'm a Grenade

Bailey Logan

I'm a grenade
A ticking time-bomb,
When the time comes I will explode,
Reducing all that is around me to rubble
We are all time bombs, grenades
Waiting for the spark,
To explode.

But does that mean we should avoid the other,
Try to leave as little of an impact as possible?
Is it better to do no harm and be forgotten?
Or to inflict harm and be remembered?
Should we tiptoe around others, holding our breath?
Or hug them, laugh, and make a connection
If we have a longer life but don't do anything have we truly lived?
Eventually our time will expire so in the time we do have shouldn't we just
    live it?
Ignore the expiration date
Love with abandon,
And live with passion.
Either way we will die
And when the time expires and we all become rubble
We won't be there to remind others of our presence,
We won't be there to remind them we lived.
Our legacy will be what they remember:
The people we helped,
The joy we spread.
So if we are alone and we never make an impact,
Do we ever really live?

I won't be alone,
Scared of my impact,
Scared of the damage I will cause.
I will love with abandon
And live with passion.
If my time expires,
I will explode,
Like I always promised I would.
 I will reduce all that is around me to rubble.
But I lived,
I was here,
And that makes it all worth it.

Cicadas

Baylina Pu

I like the way everything changes.
Moon: from blackness to borrowed light.
Cicadas: from motherland to music.
The periphery of girlhood and sweat,
ivory dawn and pull of the needle.
If I stayed here, under the magnolias,

would I remember their scent? Would they,
with their soda-can beetles and thick sweet petals,
smell like bedsheets of angels
and their Saturday-night hair
and the dust they left behind?

Seed: from secret to body.
Stone: from palm to palm.
We drove to the beach last summer,
let crushed shells dissect our feet,
let the ocean rub us raw in its scaling.

I gravitate inward, meditate under elm trees.
Flight: from silhouette to soulmate.
I'm the girl standing in the bathroom
at a party, resurrecting, soapwater maiden.
Moth: from bruise to lunar eclipse, zenith rising.

If I had been more careful,
would the future have come so soon?
Shall I light candles for her?
Should I buy last-minute supermarket flowers,
bouquet my own brain?
I should not dwell there,
make a home out of memory's
soft arms.
Energy rearranges itself,
patterns into all things.
Someday, we'll return here

marbling, piles of sediment, starry fractals
thickening the canopies,
a song rendered to stillness
by a thousand beating wings.

A First Goodbye

Cassie Hersman

The last time I was in London, the air was different. It was colder, I guess, but the atmosphere was buzzing with life. My chest was filled to the brim with anticipation at just the possibility of seeing her face again.

But the feeling I harbored now was dull. My steady heartbeat didn't feel as if it would burst through my veins and into the streets, like a love letter painted on pavement only for her.

No, it was different now.

Each step was heavy; each click, click of my heels on the pavement was my requiem. Like all great stories, they must come to an end, and just how perfect it was that it should end just where it started.

My phone buzzed against my leg, a light hum rousing me from my heavy thoughts.

K: When should I expect you?

I sighed.

G: Few minutes. On the way.

K: Cheers. xx

I stuffed my phone into my coat pocket and continued my hike across the concrete landscape.

Within minutes I was in front of her apartment, faced with the same cherry red door that divided me and what was once the tantalizing unknown.

I raised my hand to knock. I was hesitant as my knuckles met the wood, but the door was open before the thought of turning back could even cross my mind.

Kate stood in the doorframe, her tall, thin figure leaning through it with a grin that stretched from ear to ear.

As much as I wished I could ignore the way it still felt to see her, I couldn't. She was glowing. Her hazel eyes were electric, her mossy black hair framing her sculpted face like a painting.
"Hello," she greeted in her coarse morning voice.

"Hey," I replied, shifting my weight from left to right on the doormat as I forced myself to hold her gaze.

"The flat's a bit of a mess," she scratched her head and laughed sheepishly as she glanced back at the scene, "but I'm making coffee if you'd like to join me for a cup."

It took all the strength I could muster to shake my head no.

"Thank you, but I need to get going"" I explained. She arched an eyebrow. "I'm meeting a friend at noon."

She leaned her shoulder into the doorframe. I watched curiously as I saw her turn the thought over, pouting her lips out as she did when she was wagering. Noon wasn't for a few hours, and it was clear a speculation was on the tip of her tongue, ready to roll off and lure me inside. But she surprised me with a curt nod.

"I hope you have a great time," she said, a forced smile cracking her cold facade for just a moment.

"Thanks." I cleared my throat, my fingers digging into the denim of her coat for the last time. "I brought your jacket. I'm sure you've been missing it."

I held out the worn jean jacket, and Kate's eyes quickly scanned over the aged patches and nodded, taking the jacket and tucking it under her arm.

"Bye, Kate," I whispered; it was almost an apology.

"Goodbye," she answered. Not "see you soon," like it always was. Kate never wanted things to end. I wondered if she'd ever even said the word before, as the sound fell from her mouth like something of a foreign language.

I smiled softly as the door closed between us.

The Nailbiter
Anna Dove

Thirteen moons ago
As the day shook hands with the night in passing
A rabbit snuck through my garden fence.
I had seen it once or twice
Yet paid it no mind until I soon found that
The smallest thoughtless action
Can make the biggest difference
And the eternal price I was forced to pay
Left three small rows
In the weeping dirt.

One day
When the season turned
I planted seeds
As the sun bloomed
In a solemn sky.

I religiously tended to my garden
in the year that followed-
My lingering plot
That I brought forth from the earth
And buried underneath
My own name.

The flowers rise only when
I allow them to do so.
They long for my permission
And when my heart is centered
I raise my head

And they follow suit.
Purples, pinks
Blues and greens
Reflect in each of my glass eyes.

When they grow too tall-
So much so that I become lost
In my own creation
I tearfully break
Every last reaching stem
To reside with my feet.

I sit amongst
Curling petals
As the sun bakes them into a peaceful cremation.

symphonies
Aimee Straka

I used to dream of azure winds and violins - harmonies cradled my laugh and warm stars danced across slow nights like silken honey blossoming from family I snatched between static. with them I crafted smooth melodies from mist, letting safety cocoon around me like crushed velvet.

but something like ice, a pianissimo of velvet
slipped into my being, quiet beside the violins.
I kissed it away like cotton candy mist
forgetting that maybe it had etched my stars
with fractures, building its empty static
until I could not see hemlock dripping in honey.

it slid down my throat, sickly sweet honey
crawling through my veins like lyrical mist
and when I glanced in the mirror I only heard static
whispering "never enough" like discordant violins screaming their fortissimos of shattered stars, slicing me until tears dripped onto ruined velvet.

I thought that suffocating myself in velvet
would soothe my wounds, but I found honey
had been tainted and I sang fruitless hopes the stars had painted, forgetting myself in crescendos of mist and letting myself dwindle until a single violin sang its refrain to silence and I was left with static.

my eyes had been painted with desolate static, but slowly someone peeled away the coarse velvet binding my wrists and freedom appeared as violins I had erased began to drip sun warmed honey into lacerations that lingered like stubborn mist; so I chose to rewrite my arias into the stars.

and though my tears littered the ground like stars I swept them into open arms as I sat with static, realizing that sometimes concertos are lost in mist and there is a silence for every tune like velvet;
so I found my healing as slowly as cascading honey, relearning shaky adiagos on dented violins
my violins still croon imperfections to the stars but at least I now find honey in the sharpest static
and mist no longer obscures my symphonies of velvet.

Curvature: A Triptych for the Spine

Johanna Hall

inspired by Koancuts I, by Liliana Lihn

I.

in 6th grade, I failed my flexibility test in gym.
as if the universe thought a girl should be able to bend farther than her
 chubby thighs.
as if it thought not being able to touch your toes was a kind of ugliness.
(and all the stars know ugly is a war crime.)
    I am the war;
    my spine is a weapon —
    rusty. Abandoned.

my back is a glass wall —
birds fly into me when they don't believe
in the sun anymore.

my bones scabbed over the broken glass
as if they forgot healing is ugly before it is beautiful
as if the only thing this body gave me was a one-way plane ticket to self-hatred.

II.

I own a spine like a match —
the kind you can light on anything.
like the ones boys in movies strike on the back pockets of their jeans like
 being allergic to cigarettes

like boys giving you pins and needles
(and you, not being able to explain why)
like boys blowing smoke in your face and never asking or apologizing

strike me on concrete.
strike me on
a ribcage.

I used to hope I'd die alone—
for who am I to believe in the sun
when my matchstick spine won't light?

III.

there are twelve thoracic vertebrae in the middle of your spine.
    they almost hold me
    together
    they almost light me
    on fire—

what is a weapon without an enemy?
a ribcage without lungs—
a spine so brittle it
breaks?

I can touch my toes now that I
dissociate from my collarbones
when I close my eyes.
as if that's success.
as if that's something I should be proud of.

pride

light flight
like breaking glass
like denouncing smoke-blowing boys
through clenched teeth

casualties of this
war:

>   the difference between
>   holding your breath and
>   choking.
>   touching your toes and
>   servitude.

my fingertips: judge and jury
my lips a prison

I
bend
for this sentence.

Ode to Sentences
Meridith Frazee

Sometimes they are long, and you can feel the words spiral out into infinitude like the dreamy
flow of sleep.

Sometimes they are short, and waking. Ordinary. You could wear them like clothes
they are so familiar.

Inhabiting the spaces between the words,
you could float in the green, the yellow, the other watery colors left behind when the structures
wiry frames are removed leaving only
essence, diffusion.

Sometimes they burn, like the sun, like spreading pain, trickling through the nervous system like roots.

Sometimes they have the hard cold glow of the moon, of sunlight reversed and transfigured.

They can be like memories forgotten,
memories that maybe you never even had.

So quickly sliding by like fish sometimes,
that the fact of their presence is only a guess:
the memory of motion, of silver cutting water, is the only sure truth.

🌙

Sometimes they are so simple you forget they are there.
And
sometimes

they are not there at all.

Caged
Alena Masloff

My skull is an unbreakable fortress,

hiding a chaotic mind

bursting at the seams,

itching to break free.

I can't find the words to express my feelings.

Writing was supposed to be an escape,

but now I feel just as confined as before.

My mind yearns to pour all of its contents onto the page,

but it is restricted.

My vocabulary is too limited

to describe the brutal waves of chaos flooding my thoughts.

pale-lunged
Rachel Beling

it is two a.m. and the
air is heavy with the lamp's hum
and the dog's snoring and i could suffocate
if i tried. headache pressure breathed out until
i am left pale-lunged,
cells lysed. ghostly structures
like a house with memory
in every draft. pencil scratches
out bronchi, yawns carry words
to the brain. i should know how
to regenerate these lungs
from biology class. but
water is tasteless, h2o too frail,
and oxygen is potent.
if a dinosaur once drank this,
then i have tasted this moment
already. the cactus responds
to my musings with a whispered
song i've heard before. i have loved
this place enough to make it stale and sour.
that scab that fell off my chin is
still sitting in the kitchen
corner. i've lived alongside
the specks of mold contaminating
the bathroom. celebrate how we've
grown up together, blooming.
perhaps pollution is my murmured
endearment, a human kind of closeness.

in the morning, i will sigh and inhale some sun-
purified, frigid breeze. and maybe
the wind will shock my lungs into a breath
without scaffold and memory.

The Garden
Chloe Whaley

Remember
that you did not teach me not to pick flowers,
I did.
As glass streamed from my eyes and I
bled, your soul
watched and fed on my despair,
and my fingers always reaching as if to touch something
but like clouds you were
missing in action,
every frost-bitten thought that entered
my mind
killed the garden,
Remember?
The garden which you did not teach me to take care of.
The soil covered in a thick layer of
dead flowers, which had been picked prematurely
because you saw the growth and were dissatisfied.
Picking and picking and
shoveling
til the green left stains on my jeans
and your stare was burned into my hair
then my stare burned into that garden.
As darkness rose and never fell,
your laughter like pesticides sprayed on my hopes,
and you laughed and
laughed

til the day my sprouts pushed through the soil
and that glass became a safehouse around my garden.
No touching only looking,
you choose to poison us and
now,
the flowers soaked in self-love, will never be picked,
because I see the beauty and I am satisfied.
So remember
you did not teach me not to pick flowers,
I did.

Self-Worth
Sabrina Whearty

I am not good enough
I simply cannot tell myself
I create things of worth
My ideas are unoriginal
And I'm kidding myself when I say,
"You did well!"
But I mean it when I say,
"I am unworthy of praise."
No one should tell themselves,
"You are perfect the way you are."
Rather,
"You should change for others."
For this statement is untrue:
You are good enough.
(Now read from the bottom up.)

A Letter to My Parents as I'm Turning 19

Long Hoang

Dear Ma and Pa,

It's different every year but the same old me, same level of anticipation. I'm about to turn nineteen this February, and to be honest, I'm as nervous as you are. Eighteen to me contains a lot of emotion, but it went by so quickly that I didn't realize how precious the previous year was to me. During that year of being eighteen, I realized I am no longer the boy that used to hold hands with Pa; the boy he walked across the street. I'm more than capable of taking care of myself and no longer need to have Ma guide me on how to use a fork properly or remind me not to mess around with my food, or keep my table manners. Eighteen to me was a year full of fear and heartbreaking moments for me. It was the first time that I channeled all my guts to ask a girl out to dance; I was more nervous than the time I first saw the pandas at the zoo. I learned that nothing is going to work out if you don't take risks, similar to the countless nights we spent playing Dungeons and Dragons when it was a millisecond until the goblin hit me. I learned that you were right all the time. I will get to know others that will be "the one" for me, and I will know when she comes. But Pa, I think I know who is "the one" now, but do I risk it another time?

Eighteen was a year full of joy, as well. I have never thought that I would find the best friends of my life, and every day spent with them made that day even more special. I'm in a group that contains more than wonderful people. I have no words that can even describe them: Adam, who will always be there when I need to talk about my crushes; Will is my six foot eight inch gaming powerhouse buddy. I wouldn't know what to do without him. He shows me the ropes, Pa, like you do all the time; Anika is like you, Ma, always saying that I shouldn't do things that I proposed for fear that I would hurt myself. Olivia, I can always count on to be there, to talk about comics; she reminds me of you a lot, Pa; David has the sweetest soul of all. He reminds me of Lenka, how he sasses me but will always be there when I need him; Mariah, Anders, and Anna, they understand who I am better than anyone; there are many more that made this last year a whole lot better, Greg, Spencer, Edward, Sebastian, and many more, but you will have to see me in person so that I can fill you with the details.

Eighteen was also a year full of lessons, I got the chance to see what you taught me when I was just a child, and I realized how selfish of a kid I was. I learned that things might not turn out as I had imagined them to be. I had imagined the world to be so perfect, with advancement that humans now could only imagine, but it's not exactly like the dusty Lego structures I built, or the sketchy drawings with crayons I made. I'm sorry, Ma, I could not cure cancer like I told you when I was four, but I'm an artist now, and like you said, I'm happy with who I am, and I think that I will forever be when I'm able to pick up my pencils and sketch.

I realized today that those who speak more will do less, I learned it the hard way, Ma. I had always been a selfish child, I wanted things for myself and myself only, I'm loud and will speak more than what I do, but I didn't know that, at the age of eighteen, when I see my four-year-old self standing there in front of eighteen-year-old me, I know that I was wrong being selfish. I could never cure cancer and solve world hunger if I didn't have the passion to work countless hours to help people around me first. I saw my friends working alongside me and never asked for retribution. They never said a word about what they did, just like Pa. He worked tirelessly to get me and Lenka to where we are today without asking us for anything in return; all he did was to spend more time with us, and to be honest, Ma, I was blind until I realized that the prize, the happiness that I brought to others, is more valuable than what I could tangibly have in my hands.

Eighteen gave me much but also took a lot from me, as all things should be balanced. It took me away from my best friend, Grandpa. I'm now on a new journey in life, I'm now further distant from the place I used to call home. Eighteen reminds me of the time I was a kid and my hand was in Grandpa's hand. I didn't realize at the time, that stepping on the yellow painted tiles on my way to school was not as important as spending every morning with Grandpa while holding in hand a cup of hot chocolate. Eighteen was and will always be a special year for me. It took, it taught, and it gave me the tools I need for this journey I've been waiting to begin all my life--to be on my own in this world.

Love,
Your son

I Hope
Catherine Paphites

To the New Year,

I hope you bring happiness,
for those who feel as if there is no light.
I hope you bring joy,
to those who need to be fulfilled.

I hope you bring success,
for those who work their hardest.
I hope you give motivation,
to those who feel as if there is no end.

I hope you bring forgiveness,
for those who are not willing to forget.
I hope you give them the realization
that forgiving is the key to moving on.

I hope you bring acceptance,
for those who feel as if they are not enough.
I hope you bring self love and confidence,
so that we understand the beauty of humans.

I hope you bring awareness,
to our friends and communities.
I hope you help unite us,
so that we can stand strong and love one another.

I hope.

Melting Sabbath
Hewson Duffy

I.

When you wake, boundaries disappear. Snow caps
Like soft wisps of silver hair tinge the trees'
Knobbly fingers the color of glorious above,
Dissolving the barbed barrier between earth and sky.

No more must you slouch on the sidewalk, that rusty pew.
No more must you watch the slow procession of traffic,
Coughing on an exhaust pipe's counterfeit incense.
No more must you yawn listen to the rubber choir honk tin melodies.
No more must you stare as salvation is reduced to glaring headlights:
The street is empty.

Reclaim the frozen morning.
Let the snowflakes drifting into your hair baptise you.
Seize the clouds as rosary beads and pray
That you might sled down scripture's bumpy parables,
Might dance in a cathedral domed only in night.
Peace be with the invisible—the inaudible—
This imprecise perfection. Eucharist is nothing
If not crystallized symmetry landing
On your outstretched tongue.

II.

Earthy afternoon colors bleeding through the immaculate, Patches of
 grassy temptation poking through the snow, and Sledding tracks reveal-
 ing muddy foundations. Was it all a facade, this temple inside out,
This blizzard hush, this melting sabbath?

III.

Tomorrow you'll forget what's beyond
The buzzing sludge that clogs your ears.
And later, when your shuffling boots again stick
To the sidewalk, and Wednesday sun shoves
The sky out of the way, and the last wistful flurries Float onto your forehead
 like alabaster ashes,
You'll brush them off impatiently, for the barbed wire—
Border between brittle branch ends and infinite blue— Will have finally
 resolidified.

Clarisse

Niav Condron

Clarisse was born in Chamonix, France, but longed to go further. The tiny town on the French border of Switzerland was home to the ski tourists filtering in from neighboring countries, not to her. She wanted to go beyond her snow-filled boots, her frostbitten nose, the ancient soapstone fireplace in her guest room she spent hours huddled near, wishing for a warmer climate.

Clarisse is old now, older than the ancient woman she used to buy eggs from in the market on Sundays. She looks in the mirror and sees the lines of wrinkles across her forehead, her skin warped from decades of stress and toil. She remembers seeing the brightly colored magazines in the department store next to her house when she was nine, photos of women in floral swimsuits posing on a sandy beach with crystalline water plastered across the pages. She was enamored with the tropical setting, enough to buy a swimsuit and sneak out of her house that night to a nearby lake. It was at the peak of winter, and the lake had frozen over, so she brought an axe to break the ice and reach what she thought would be warm water. Nevertheless, she fell through, and when she woke up, she was in a hospital bed in Paris, her mother clutching her ice blue hand.

Everything changed when her father died when she was 16 and her mother became distant. Clarisse began to sneak out more often, not in hopes of finding a beach in the cold

climate of Eastern France, but to see boys. It wasn't so much of a problem until her mother got a call from the doctor. Clarisse's baby boy was born that summer when the weather wasn't so frigid, hence the name June. Long gone from living in her mother's house, now taking refuge in a women's shelter four hours away in Switzerland. She cherished June more than she adored the fragrance of the alpine meadow flowers that a warm breeze occasionally brought through her window.

When June was six, they moved. Clarisse thought it was too dangerous to raise a child in war-torn Europe and that he would find a better education in

America. They took refuge in New York City where June started in the first grade, while she worked in a laundromat. With no knowledge of the English language. June dropped out of school. She lost her job when she burnt a hole in the shirt of a prestigious customer. With no income, they had no home.

The bustling streets of the city gave her a thrill like no other. She stole bread from the bakery and milk from the man with the cows. She felt remorse from stealing, but gained back the gratitude when she saw June giggle as she said, "You grow big and strong. Like bull." It was the only English the two knew, after hearing the Russian butcher in Central Park say it. She was going to miss the city, but she needed a job.

And then she finally did it. Scraped together to buy enough money for two train tickets to Miami, Florida. She got a job, June went back to school, and she bought an apartment

overlooking the shoreline. She woke up to the sounds of her son's excited squeals as he got ready for his day at school and fell asleep to the monotone whoosh of the waves as it touched the shore.

Clarisse sits in her rocking chair, recollecting on her childhood. She remembers the icy sting of the water when she fell in, the intense pain in her lower body when she gave birth to June, the feeling of the crisp summer breeze of Switzerland that occasionally blew through her window and the rubbing of her shoes against her heels as she walked about New York City.

She then remembers the excitement she experienced when she moved to Miami; how she was able to see a beach for the first time. She remembers how happy she was when her baby boy was born, how gratifying it felt to hold his tiny head in her hand.

Clarisse's life wasn't easy. And for that, she loved it.

"All this pain," Clarisse says to herself. "And yet so much joy." She then shuts her eyes and falls into a deep, deep sleep.

growing pains
Maryam Alwan

Every time i look at a child, i get an inexplicable sad feeling—
all i can see is the person they'll become,
the protective bubble of innocence that surrounds them
bursting.

i want to shield them from the cold shock of diving into reality's deep end;
i want to capture the light in their eyes and keep it from leaking out.

they are fresh sheets of pristine, pure paper waiting to be scribbled on,
and i'm watching a movie that's been played billions of times before,
and i know how it ends,
but i can't do anything about it.

annoying boys turn into men you have to keep your guard up around
and playground bullies grow up to be corporate assholes.
i guess every murderer was a kid once, too—
and that's what frightens me.

remember thinking your parents could do no wrong?
the day i found out my dad cheated is still carved in my memory.

remember excitedly drawing shaky marker lines on the wall for every inch gained?
the concept of growth and adulthood are no longer alluring, they're terrifying.

now, i watch as milestones i imagined reaching as a kid are ticked off
one
after
another

˙☾˙

and i'm wondering how romanticized dreams can so easily become
    nightmareish actuality.

17 is the age sung about at the top of the charts and splayed across the CW;
my friends are all being given cars and finding jobs and getting recruited
    by colleges
and here i am too scared to do Driver's Ed,
because it would be the final nail in the coffin of my childhood.

breathe your cigarette smoke into my lungs
and choke away the non-stop playback of the years
i've been told that time flies by my whole life,
but this is the first time i've felt the whiplash.

how is it that i feel exactly the same as i did a decade ago,
but because my body has matured, it's expected that i have, too?

teen years are a scary thing—
you go in as a 12-year-old and come out an adult;
you take it week by week and, suddenly, years have passed.

take me back to coloring outside the lines,
to coloring books filled with purple grass and blue people,
to aspirations of astronauts and fifty careers at once,
before we were told who to be.

i suppose this feeling will just intensify as i get older—
i'll look in the mirror and see the same wide eyes that stared back at me
    50 years ago;
i'll place my weathered palm on my chest and feel the same beat that
    played in the womb;
i'll be slowly whisked away like the generations before me.

Maybe Peter Pan had the right idea.

a list
McKenzie Hall

2005 smiling is sweet and laughter comes easily and life can only be described as truly good

2009 i do not know shakespeare but i do know the world is my stage i start a list of things i can be it reads: anything

2012 the world grows bigger while i grow smaller and my mother's car smells like hairspray and fear so i

write a list of ways to make friends and i am told to write: be myself but any eleven year old knows that is never enough

2015 i am too loud and i try to list all the things that could go wrong and i end up shaking but if i smile bigger and shine brighter i can still be perfect and this is just how life
is

2016 it turns out pain is an explosive and all of a sudden i am drowning in oxygen i forget that being a woman is not being small and i write a list of things i can be it reads:
nothing

2017 i repeat "this too shall pass" until it passes this is the refrain of my life i have learned square roots and insignificance but not how to cope i can't help but wonder if smiling has always covered bruised insides and i am only just now feeling it or if life was ever truly good because i don't remember not feeling like
this

2018 i am relearning to love running
because muscle aches are no longer the most painful thing
and i am relearning to pray because seventeen years of faith are becoming
rote and i am relearning that i need prayer to heal the more painful things
because i have tried by myself and it is
killing me and i was never made to be
alone

2019 and i am not healed yet but i am
teaching myself breathing and trust in and out and in and out and hope
and maybe life will be truly good again

About Our Editors

Baylina Pu *Editor-in-Chief*
Baylina Pu has been telling stories her whole life. She is co-editor-in-chief of Albemarle High School's literary-art magazine, The Lantern, and has attended the Virginia Governor's School for the Humanities as well as the University of Virginia Young Writers Workshop. Her writing has been awarded nationally by the Scholastic Art & Writing Awards among other honors, and her aspirations include studying literature from cultures around the world, publishing novels and poetry collections, and collaborating on wide-reaching projects with other artists. In addition to writing poetry and fiction, she enjoys art, music, performing, and making puns. This is Baylina's third year volunteering with the Tupelo Press Teen Writing Center.

Rachel Beling *Advisor and Editor*
Rachel Beling is a senior at Charlottesville High School, where she has served as the editor of Graffiti, the school's literary magazine. She has volunteered with the Tupelo Press Teen Writing Center for three year and was the managing editor for the Crossroads VI Teen Anthology. In 2018, Rachel attended the Virginia Governor's School for the Humanities and received the Arthur C. Greene Rising Star Award in Writing. She shares her passion for words with her community by tutoring English as a Second Language students and by providing books through her Little Free Library. She looks forward to sharing her enthusiasm for writing with her college peers next year.

Astrid Weisend *Proof Reader and Editor*
Astrid Weisend is a senior at Albemarle High School who particularly enjoys fiction writing. Astrid has been involved with The Lantern, an award winning high school litmag, and volunteered as an editor and proofreader for the Crossroads Teen Anthology for two years. Astrid is an excellent proofreader,

and invaluable team member of any organization she sets her hand to. She is trying to get into college, while also making the best of her last year in high school and attempting to avoid sports injuries.

Mary Dwyer *Managing Editor*

Mary Dwyer is a long time writer who has really intensified her commitment to the craft in high school. Joining the Tupelo Press Teen Writing Center has given her more time to explore her voice. Mary has volunteered with the Albemarle High School litmag, the Lantern, and the Tupelo Press Teen Writing Center as an editor, organizer, and proofreader. She enjoys all forms of writing but her forte is poetry, with several published pieces. She looks forward to pursuing this into her adulthood, as she could not imagine a future without writing in it. Besides writing, Mary enjoys filming movies and coaching synchronized swimming.

Chloe Whaley *Editor-at-large*

Chloe Whaley is a senior at Albemarle High School. She has been taking creative writing since seventh grade, and has been a part of the Literary Arts Magazine at AHS for three years. Chloe was the co-editor-in-chief of the Tupelo Press Teen Writing Center Instagram account for the 2017/2018 school year, and a strong contributor to the editorial staff. In her free time she enjoys playing volleyball, hiking, and eating food. She also enjoys spending time with her three younger siblings and loves baking with them.

Stella Rowe *Editor*

Stella Rowe is a sophomore at Western Albemarle High School who finds joy in the art of sharing stories with others and in experimenting with various writing styles. She aspires to take inspiration from every area of life and to reach others through her writing. Stella enjoys theater and film and loves to sing, play the guitar and write songs. She hopes to expand her knowledge of literature and art and to always create.

Abigail Connelly *Editor*

Abigail Connelly is a sophomore at Western Albemarle High School. She is a staff member of the school newspaper and works as copy editor, also writing occasionally for the opinion section. Abigail loves to read and write and has a particular fondness for poetry and short stories. This is her third year with the Writer House summer camp program. Outside of reading and writing, Abigail loves to compose music, hike, climb, and ride bikes.

Natasha Levine *Junior Editor*

Natasha Levine is a eighth grader at Tandem Friends School who particularly likes fiction writing. Natasha previously wrote and edited a monthly newsletter for her neighborhood and this is her first year at the Tupelo Press Teen Writing Center. In her free time she enjoys reading, writing and photography.

www.ingramcontent.com/pod-product-compliance
Lightning Source LLC
Chambersburg PA
CBHW021951290426
44108CB00012B/1027